Mary Berry's
FOOD PROCESSOR COOKBOOK

Mary Berry's FOOD PROCESSOR COOKBOOK

PIATKUS

How lucky I have been to have had Joanna Drew to help me with this book. Joanna has used a processor for over 10 years, and has the added bonus of a professional cookery training. She is an inventive cook and dear friend. My special thanks to her.

© 1990 Mary Berry

First published in 1990 by
Judy Piatkus (Publishers) Ltd
5 Windmill Street, London W1P 1HF

British Library Cataloguing in Publication Data
Berry, Mary, *1935–*
    Mary Berry's food processor cookbook.
    1. Food: Dishes prepared using food processors – recipes
    I. Title
    641.5'89

    ISBN 0 86188–957–6

Edited by Wendy Toole
Designed by Paul Saunders
Illustrations by Paul Saunders
Photography by James Murphy
Styling by Sarah Wiley

Typeset in 11/13 Linotron Sabon by
Phoenix Photosetting, Chatham, Kent
Printed and bound in Great Britain at
The Bath Press, Bath, Avon

Contents

Introduction

The food processor has been an essential part of my kitchen for more than twenty years. It is not tucked away under a worktop. It is out at the ready. The more I use my processor, the more uses I find for it!

I use it to speed up my family cooking as well as when cooking for special occasions. It does the laborious tasks which until I had a processor I did by hand, such as mincing meat (what a bore to get out the mincer, then wash it up) and slicing cucumber. It makes breadcrumbs, pastry, pâtés, cakes mixes, mayonnaise and dressing in seconds — all things which I make often and which without a processor take time. I hope that the recipes I have included in this book will show you just how versatile and timesaving it can be.

I am crafty: I plan its use carefully so I don't have to wash up the bowl more often than necessary. I start by doing, say, crumble mix, then breadcrumbs, and follow on with a meat pâté. There is no need to wash up in between, which of course you would have to do if you did the same jobs in reverse. Always think what you want to use it for and plan accordingly. If you do need to clean it quickly, pour in a little hot water and switch it on for a few moments to rinse the bowl clean.

Food processors save time and effort, slicing vegetables beautifully or mixing pastry in seconds. They also cut down on waste. Take cold leftover jacket potatoes for example. They can be given a new lease of life as Thatched Potatoes (page 62), when potatoes are mashed with herbs and butter and given a crunchy topping made from the shredded potato skins crispened in the oven and mixed with grated cheese. A few leftover lightly-cooked fresh vegetables can be made into a nutritious soup for two — just process with a

little leftover good gravy, if you have it, and make up to 1 pint (600 ml) with stock. For added flavour, add a squeeze of tomato purée.

For the quickest ever kofta-style meatballs, take the last trimmings from the Sunday joint — lamb is best — and process with a little onion, a few sprigs of parsley, some ground cumin and coriander, salt, pepper and a spoonful or two of yoghurt. Roll into small balls the size of walnuts and fry gently in butter and oil until golden.

All these recipes for this book were tested in my Magimix. However, they will work just as well in any other type of food processor.

Getting the best out of the processor if you're used to a blender

Most blenders consist of a tall goblet-shaped container with blades in the base. They have neither the capacity nor the power of a processor. Blenders work best with a good proportion of liquid to solids, whereas a processor is most efficient when the contents are fairly dry. For example, if using a blender you would drop parsley or other herbs into liquid when making a sauce. In a processor, the herbs would chop better without any added liquid. Always strain off excess liquid before processing.

Attachments

The recipes in this book use only the basic blades and discs that come with all food processors. I have not included recipes using juice extractors or the various chip-makers, whisks and so forth which come with some machines.

The discs I have used are the ones that I find most useful: fine and coarse slicing and grating discs. Some machines have only one grade of grating disc, while others have also a very fine 'Parmesan' grater. Use the most appropriate one for the recipe.

Some processor manufacturers offer whisks, but to be honest I would prefer to buy an inexpensive hand-held electric whisk. You can even take it to the pan if you have a lumpy sauce!

All the bowls, blades and discs on machines I have used have been dishwasher-proof on a low temperature. Check with your own model.

Dangers

Overprocessing

One of the greatest dangers with a food processor is overprocessing. Always slightly underprocess, then check. You can switch on for a moment more if necessary but you cannot go backwards.

Pâtés: If you are processing liver you naturally want it to be as smooth as possible, and it should literally go down to a pouring consistency. But if you are adding ham or bacon to make a coarser pâté, process in short bursts and watch the texture carefully. You don't want a purée!

Soups: With a vegetable soup, don't always purée until totally velvet-smooth — sometimes leave it chunky. Many people feel that a soup is better with a little fibre and texture.

Vegetable purées: Mashed potato is not successful unless done with enormous care because it quickly becomes gluey, but other vegetable purées — such as celeriac, swede,

carrot, parsnip, or a mixture of these — work very well. You will find Brussels sprout purée is better if you underprocess slightly so that you still get the texture of the sprouts.

Onions: Be careful not to overprocess when chopping raw onions. They will go mushy.

Cakes and doughs: It is very important not to overprocess cakes or pastry. Pastry becomes tough and leathery and will shrink. If you overprocess cakes it will affect the rising, and again they will be tough.

Crumble: If you overprocess crumble it will form pastry without any added liquid, but you won't be able to use it as pastry because it will be too difficult to handle and impossible to roll out. If this does happen, don't be tempted to add more flour to turn it back into a crumble because the mixture won't be rich enough. Instead, put the lump in a plastic bag in the freezer for 30 minutes or so, then grate it using the coarse grating disc.

Overfilling

Underfill rather than overfill the processor bowl. It's much better to do a couple of batches than have liquid dripping out of the bowl all over the worktop. When making cakes or bread, don't strain the machine by trying to do too much at a time.

Basic techniques in the processor

Baby food

Home-made cooked meals can be simply puréed in the processor. The bowl and the blade can be sterilised with Milton, too.

Breadcrumbs

Process crusts and crumbs separately. Use the best breadcrumbs for bread sauce and special recipes; the crusts crumbed are fine for stuffings and for coating. Keep brown and white crumbs separately in the freezer.

Cheese
Grate odd pieces of leftover cheese. Keep in the freezer until needed.

Crumbles and pastry
They work best using cold fat.

Curry powder
With a processor you can create exciting new curry flavours in seconds. Make curry powder in smallish amounts and store in a screw-top jar, and always write down the proportions of spices you use so you can duplicate a really good combination. Try a mixture of 4 parts whole coriander, 2 parts cummin seed and 1 part cardomom and add a little chilli powder if you like a hotter curry. Some ground turmeric can also be added to give the traditional yellow colour. Do experiment!

Custard for trifles
Make very thick packet-mix custard, then cool and process. The result will be a pale custard which will set like a gentle jelly on top of a trifle.

French dressing
Make a quantity in the processor, then keep in a cool place for up to three weeks.

Icing and buttercream
When making a quantity of icing or buttercream it is amazingly quick in the processor, and guaranteed free from lumps.

Lemons
Slice small or halved large lemons for drinks and keep in a plastic box in the refrigerator for up to three days, or freeze.

Low-calorie meals
Interesting salads of different textures of sliced and grated vegetables can be prepared in the processor. Also yoghurt and lemon-based non-fattening dressings can be created with little effort. Fresh fruit can be processed and sieved, if necessary, then stirred into low-fat yoghurt. Vegetables and fruit can be puréed to make drinks.

Nuts
If you often use chopped nuts for cooking, chop a quantity at one go. Put in polybags and freeze – chopped nuts keep for two years in the freezer.

Parsley
Chop a quantity at a time. Keep in a plastic box in the freezer and just scrape out a spoonful without thawing whenever you need it.

Sauces and soups
For the smoothest sauces and soups, strain off the liquid and process only the chunky pieces. Then mix the purée into the liquid.

Sieving
Fresh and stewed fruits that need to be sieved for fools or mousses – such as raspberries, loganberries, blackberries and gooseberries – go through the sieve far more quickly and with a higher yield if processed first.

Slicing vegetables
The essential thing is to get the vegetables lined up, vertical and straight, in the feed tube so you get regular slices. Push down on the plastic pusher with even pressure, keeping a watchful eye on what you're doing. This particularly applies to carrots and potatoes.

Pâtés and First Courses

Pâtés are easy to make in the processor. Don't be tempted to put all the ingredients in the bowl at one go in every recipe or you will always end up with pâtés of the same smooth texture. Liver pâtés need to be smooth, but pâtés containing other meats and game are far more interesting if left fairly chunky.

To give a pâté a good flavour and consistency you need to add fat. Smoked fish pâtés aren't cooked and you can use a low-fat spread instead of butter in these if you prefer. You can also use a low-fat soft cheese instead of cream cheese, but don't be disappointed if the flavour is not the same.

Low-fat spreads contain a lot of added water. The fat and water separate when they are heated, so you can't use them in pâtés that need to be cooked. For these pâtés use a full fat such as butter which has a very low water content.

Fish pâtés are the best to make ahead as they freeze so well.

A Pâté of Three Smoked Fishes

◆

SERVES 6–8

A wonderful layered pâté. The smoked salmon can be just odd pieces or the last cuts. Serve the pâté with Melba toast or crisp warm toast and butter.

about 4 oz (100 g) smoked salmon slices

TROUT PÂTÉ
3 oz (75 g) smoked trout, skinned and boned
1½ oz (40 g) butter, softened, or low-fat spread
1½ oz (40 g) cream cheese
2 teaspoons lemon juice
salt
freshly ground black pepper

SALMON PÂTÉ
2 oz (50 g) smoked salmon pieces
1 oz (25 g) butter, softened, or low-fat spread
1 oz (25 g) cream cheese
2 teaspoons lemon juice
2 teaspoons tomato purée
salt
freshly ground black pepper

MACKEREL PÂTÉ
3 oz (75 g) smoked mackerel fillets, skinned
1½ oz (40 g) butter, softened
1½ oz (40 g) cream cheese
2 teaspoons lemon juice
salt
freshly ground black pepper

USING THE METAL BLADE

Line a 1 pint (600 ml) terrine or loaf tin with clear film, letting the edges overhang. Line with smoked salmon slices, saving a few for the top.

For the trout pâté, measure all the ingredients into the processor bowl and process until smooth. Scrape down the sides of the bowl and briefly reprocess. Turn into the prepared terrine and level off the top, then stand the terrine in the refrigerator while you prepare the next layer of pâté. There is no need to wash out the bowl between layers.

Process the ingredients for the salmon pâté in the same way and spread on top of the trout pâté.

Finally, process the ingredients for the mackerel pâté and spread it on top of the salmon pâté. Cover with the remaining smoked salmon slices, wrap the overhanging edges of clear film over the top and chill overnight.

To serve, turn out and slice while very cold.

Kipper Pâté

SERVES 6

Kippers are inexpensive and make an excellent pâté. They need to be cooked first (see method). Don't be tempted to add the cream to the kipper mixture in the processor: you get a lighter more mousse-like effect by whipping the cream separately. Serve the pâté with hot toast.

6 oz (175 g) packet frozen boil-in-the-bag kipper fillets
a little lemon juice
freshly ground black pepper
¼ pint (150 ml) double cream
parsley and lemon wedges, for garnish

USING THE METAL BLADE

Cook the kippers according to the directions on the packet, then leave until cool enough to handle. Remove black skins and process the fillets with the lemon juice and plenty of black pepper. Continue until the mixture is smooth. Scrape down the sides of the bowl and process briefly.

Measure the cream into a bowl and whip until it forms soft peaks, then gently fold the processed fish into the cream and mix well. Turn into six small individual dishes and refrigerate until needed. Garnish with parsley and a wedge of lemon to serve.

Mackerel Pâté

SERVES 6

Low-fat spread can be used instead of butter in this recipe as the fat does not need to be heated. Using low-fat soft cheese instead of cream cheese means that the end result is a tasty pâté that's low in calories.

8 oz (225 g) smoked mackerel fillets, skinned
4 oz (100 g) butter
4 oz (100 g) low-fat soft cheese
1 tablespoon capers
1 tablespoon lemon juice
freshly ground black pepper

USING THE METAL BLADE

Measure all the ingredients into the processor bowl and process until smooth. Scrape down the sides of the bowl and briefly reprocess.

Turn into a small terrine and chill until set. Serve with brown toast.

Sardine-Stuffed Lemons

SERVES 4

A smart first course. Serve on individual plates with hot buttered toast or crusty French bread and butter.

> *4 small lemons*
> *2 oz (50 g) butter, softened*
> *2 oz (50 g) cream cheese*
> *4½ oz (125 g) can sardines in oil or brine, drained*
> *freshly ground black pepper*
> *4 fresh bay leaves, for garnish*

USING THE METAL BLADE

With a sharp knife, cut a thin slice from the base of each lemon so that they stand flat. Cut and reserve a larger slice from the top of each lemon. Scoop out the flesh from the body of the lemons using a serrated or grapefruit knife and strain through a sieve. Reserve the juice and discard the flesh.

Measure the butter and cheese into the processor bowl and add the sardines. Pour in some of the lemon juice and a generous sprinkling of black pepper. Process until all the ingredients are well mixed but not too smooth, then scrape down the sides of the bowl and add more lemon juice if needed. Check seasoning. Spoon the mixture into the lemons and sit the lids on top.

To serve, garnish each lemon with a fresh bay leaf.

Variation

Quick Sardine Pâté

Make the pâté as above using the juice of just one small lemon. Instead of packing the pâté into lemon shells, simply divide between four small ramekin dishes or spoon into a small serving dish. Level the surface and decorate with a bay leaf.

Highland Game Pâté

◆

SERVES 6

Frozen pigeon is now available throughout the year and is quite inexpensive. If you're lucky enough to be given other game such as aged pheasant or some venison, then that could be used instead. To check seasoning once the pâté is made, fry a spoonful of the mixture lightly in oil until cooked, then taste and add more pepper and salt as needed.

MARINADE
⅛ pint (75 ml) wine
⅛ pint (75 ml) oil
salt
freshly ground black pepper
1 small onion, sliced

8 oz (225 g) boned raw pigeon breasts
1 slice brown bread
8 oz (225 g) belly pork
8 oz (225 g) piece fatty bacon
8 oz (225 g) chicken livers
1 egg
salt
freshly ground black pepper
2 cloves garlic, crushed
scant level teaspoon grated nutmeg
3 tablespoons snipped fresh chives
a little melted butter
bay leaves, for garnish

USING THE METAL BLADE

Mix together the ingredients for the marinade in a bowl. Soak the pigeon breasts in the marinade overnight.

Next day, remove the meat from the marinade. Strain the marinade and soak the bread in it. Heat the oven to 350°F/180°C/gas mark 4 and butter a 2 pint (1.2 litre) terrine.

Process the meats one at a time. With the exception of the chicken livers, which should be puréed, make sure the meats are not minced too finely. Process the soaked bread with one of the meats. In a bowl mix together all the prepared meats, the remaining marinade, the egg, salt, pepper, garlic, nutmeg and chives. Mix well and turn into the terrine. Cover with a lid or foil, stand in a roasting tin and pour in hot water to come half way up the side of the terrine. Bake in the oven for about 2 hours, until when pierced with a fine skewer the juices that run out are practically clear.

Cool for several hours, then pour on the melted butter and garnish with a bay leaf or two.

Rillettes de Porc

SERVES 6–8

Traditional French potted meat made from belly pork. In the country districts of France, where this was originally made, the cooked meat was shredded laboriously using two forks, but with care a superb result can be made in the processor.

> 2 lb (900 g) boneless belly of pork, rind removed, cut into
>   smallish chunks
> 3 tablespoons sherry
> bunch of fresh thyme
> 3 cloves
> 1/2 teaspoon grated nutmeg
> 2 cloves garlic, crushed
> salt
> freshly ground black pepper
> 2 oz (50 g) butter
> sprigs of thyme, for garnish

USING THE METAL BLADE

Heat the oven to 325°F/160°C/gas mark 3. Put the pork in a flameproof casserole with the sherry, thyme, cloves, nutmeg, garlic and seasoning and bring to the boil. Cover the casserole with a lid, then transfer to the oven and cook for about 3 hours, until the meat falls apart.

Remove the thyme and cloves and transfer half the meat to the processor bowl. Shred it in short bursts, taking care not to overprocess: you should still be able to see the meat fibres. Turn the processed meat into a bowl and repeat with the remaining meat. Combine the two batches and check seasoning.

Divide the mixture among 6–8 ramekins or turn it into a terrine. Pour over any liquid from the casserole then chill until set. Melt the butter and pour it over the pork mixture. Leave to set. Garnish with thyme sprigs to serve.

Smoked Salmon Mousses

SERVES 6

This wonderful starter is a light mousse encased in smoked salmon. Served with a dill-flavoured sauce (page 68) it makes a most impressive beginning to a meal. It does take a little time to prepare the individual ramekins but the effort is well worth it. Leave out the prawns, if you prefer.

about 8 oz (225 g) sliced smoked salmon
6 oz (175 g) smoked salmon pieces
2 oz (50 g) butter, softened
2 oz (50 g) cream cheese
5 oz (150 g) Greek yoghurt
1 tablespoon tomato purée
juice of ½ lemon
salt
freshly ground black pepper
3 oz (75 g) shelled prawns
sprigs of dill or parsley and sliced cucumber, for garnish

USING THE METAL BLADE

Turn six ramekins upside down and cover the outside of each with clear film. Next, cover the dishes with a layer of sliced smoked salmon, overlapping the pieces if necessary to make sure there are no gaps. Then cover the smoked salmon with another layer of clear film. Very carefully remove the three layers, keeping the shape intact, and drop gently inside the ramekins. Press in well and reshape slightly to fit. Remove the top layer of clear film and set the salmon-lined moulds aside, ready to fill with mousse.

Measure all the remaining ingredients except the prawns, dill or parsley and cucumber into the processor bowl and process until smooth. Scrape down the sides and briefly reprocess, then taste and check seasoning. Add the prawns and carefully process just long enough to mix them in. Spoon the mixture into the moulds and chill in the refrigerator for at least 4 hours.

To serve, invert the ramekins on serving plates, lift off the moulds and remove the clear film. Decorate with sprigs of dill or parsley and slices of cucumber.

FACING PAGE: *A Pâté of Three Smoked Fishes (page 11)*

OPPOSITE PAGE 17, LEFT: *Chicken and Watercress Raised Pie (page 48)*, RIGHT: *English Lamb Stuffed with Watercress and Ham (page 43)*

Avocado Mousse with Prawn Mayonnaise

SERVES 8–10

Serve this pretty green and pink first course with slices of brown bread and butter or small brown rolls.

¾ oz (20 g) powdered gelatine
¼ pint (150 ml) good chicken stock
2 large ripe avocado pears
juice of ½ lemon
½ pint (300 ml) mayonnaise (page 67)
salt
freshly ground black pepper
¼ pint (150 ml) double cream, lightly whipped
watercress or cress, for garnish

PRAWN MAYONNAISE
8 oz (225 g) shelled prawns, well drained
½ pint (300 ml) mayonnaise (page 67)
2 teaspoons tomato purée
a little Worcestershire sauce
juice of ½ lemon
1 teaspoon creamed horseradish
freshly ground black pepper

USING THE METAL BLADE

Measure the gelatine into a bowl and mix with 6 tablespoons of the cold stock. Leave for 5 minutes to form a sponge. Stand the bowl in a pan of simmering water until the gelatine has dissolved and the liquid is clear. Stir the gelatine solution into the remaining stock.

Halve the avocados, remove the stones and peel. Put the flesh into the processor bowl, add the stock, lemon juice, mayonnaise and seasoning and process until smooth. Add the cream and process for a few moments, until blended evenly. Check seasoning.

Oil a 2 pint (1.2 litre) ring mould. Pour the mixture into the mould, cover with clear film and chill overnight.

Mix together all the ingredients for the prawn mayonnaise in a bowl, first making sure that the prawns are really well drained. Check seasoning.

To turn out the mousse, dip the mould in a bowl of very hot water for a moment to loosen it. Place a damp serving plate on top, then invert the mould on to the plate. Lift off the mould. Fill the centre of the mousse with the prawn mayonnaise and serve garnished with watercress sprigs or cress.

Brandied Liver Pâté

SERVES 6

This is such an easy pâté to make and is full of flavours. Expect the centre of it to be pale pink. Serve with warm toast and butter.

1 small onion, cut into quarters
6 oz (175 g) butter, melted
1 lb (450 g) chicken livers
4 tablespoons brandy
1 fat clove garlic, crushed
leaves from 2 sprigs fresh marjoram
salt
freshly ground black pepper
sprigs of fresh herbs, for garnish

USING THE METAL BLADE

Heat the oven to 350°F/180°C/gas mark 4 and well grease a 1 lb (450 g) terrine or tin.

Process the onion until finely chopped, add the butter, livers, brandy, garlic, marjoram and seasoning and process until smooth. Transfer the contents of the processor to the terrine and cover with a lid or foil. Stand in a roasting tin and pour in boiling water to come half way up the side of the terrine, then bake in the oven for about 40 minutes, until firm to the touch in the centre.

Cool, then leave in the refrigerator until chilled. To serve, turn out and decorate with sprigs of fresh herbs.

Herb Spinach Terrine

SERVES 4

If serving this cold, mix together equal quantities of yoghurt and French dressing to make a light sauce to go with it. This terrine mixture is also an excellent filling for a quiche.

4 oz (100 g) farmhouse Cheddar
1 lb (450 g) frozen leaf spinach, thawed and well drained
small bunch chives, snipped
4 eggs
½ pint (300 ml) single cream
salt
freshly ground black pepper

USING THE COARSE
GRATING DISC:
METAL BLADE

Heat the oven to 350°F/180°C/gas mark 4. Lightly grease a 2 lb (900 g) loaf tin and put a piece of baking parchment in the bottom.

Grate the cheese in the processor, then tip into a bowl and keep on one side. Fit the metal blade and process the spinach for a few seconds until roughly chopped. Then add the chives, eggs, cream, cheese and seasoning and process until well blended.

Pour the mixture into the loaf tin. Stand in a roasting tin and pour in hot water to come half way up the side of the loaf tin. Carefully lift into the oven and cook for about 1 hour, until set.

Leave to cool slightly then turn out the terrine on to a plate. Serve either warm or cold, in slices.

Taramasalata

SERVES 6

A Greek pâté-cum-dip made from smoked cod's roe, which is a lovely pink colour. Do go carefully with the salt as the smoked roe can be very salty already. Roes are available from fishmongers and supermarkets, but failing that they are available in jars from good delicatessens. Serve with warmed pitta bread or hot toast.

> *2 small slices white bread, crusts removed*
> *2 tablespoons milk*
> *8 oz (225 g) smoked cod's roe, skinned*
> *1 clove garlic, crushed (optional)*
> *4 fl oz (120 ml) oil*
> *2 tablespoons lemon juice*
> *salt*
> *freshly ground black pepper*
> *parsley sprigs, for garnish*

USING THE METAL
BLADE

Soak the bread in the milk, then squeeze out as much milk as possible.

Process the cod's roe to a fine paste, add the bread, and the garlic if using, and process again. With the motor running, trickle in the oil through the funnel until it is all absorbed. Add the lemon juice and season to taste. Turn into a small dish and chill thoroughly.

Serve garnished with sprigs of parsley.

Aubergine Caviar

SERVES 6

An unusual appetizer served with hot toast. Alternatively, use it to fill seeded, skinned tomato cups.

1 large onion, cut into quarters
6 tablespoons olive oil
2 large aubergines, cut into quarters
1 small green pepper, seeded
1 fat clove garlic, crushed
salt
freshly ground black pepper
lemon juice

USING THE METAL BLADE

Chop the onion in the processor. Heat the oil in a large pan, add the onion and soften for 5 minutes.

Process the aubergines and green pepper briefly and add to the pan with the garlic. Cook over a gentle heat until the vegetables are just tender and the mixture is thick. Most of the juice should have evaporated.

Tip the contents of the pan into the processor bowl and process for a short time, stopping when the mixture still has a slight texture to it. Check seasoning and add a little lemon juice. Chill thoroughly in the refrigerator before serving.

Hummus

SERVES 10

Originally from Greece, this delicious dip is very quickly prepared in the processor. Once you have made it at home you won't ever bother to buy it from supermarkets, not just because it's easy to make but because the flavour is much nicer. Serve as a dip with raw vegetable sticks or warm pitta bread. You can use canned or frozen chick peas, which will cut down the preparation time: you would need 1 lb (450 g) drained canned chick peas as they double in weight when soaked and cooked.

8 oz (225 g) dried chick peas
3 fat cloves garlic, crushed
3 tablespoons lemon juice
3 tablespoons oil
2 tablespoons tahini
salt
freshly ground black pepper

USING THE METAL BLADE

Soak the chick peas overnight in a bowl of cold water.

Next day drain the chick peas, put them in a saucepan with enough cold water to cover them by about 3 inches (7.5 cm) and bring to the boil. Do not add salt at this stage as it tends to toughen the skins. Simmer for 1–1½ hours, until tender, then leave to cool in their cooking liquid.

Measure the garlic, lemon juice, oil, tahini and drained chick peas into the processor and process until smooth. Add a tablespoon or two of the chick-pea cooking liquid or water to thin the mixture a little, if necessary. Scrape down the sides of the bowl and process until you have the consistency you like. Add plenty of seasoning, then reprocess briefly. Transfer the hummus to a serving bowl.

Courgette Flowers with Salmon Mousse

SERVES 6

These fragile flowers make unusual cases for the salmon mousse. Worth the effort of deep frying, they need to be served as soon as possible afterwards. Serve as a light first course.

BATTER
4 oz (100 g) flour
¼ pint (150 ml) water
1 tablespoon oil

12 courgette flowers
8 oz (250 g) raw fresh salmon, skinned, boned and roughly cut
1 egg white
salt
freshly ground black pepper
¼ pint (150 ml) double cream
oil for deep frying

USING THE METAL BLADE

Measure all the ingredients for the batter into the processor bowl and process until smooth. Pour into a jug and set aside.

Gently open the courgette flowers. Trim the stamen and most of the stalk.

To make the mousse, measure the salmon, egg white and seasoning into the processor bowl and process until smooth. With the machine running, add the cream through the funnel. Be careful not to overprocess. Transfer the mousse to a bowl, cover and chill thoroughly before using.

To serve, carefully put a teaspoon of mousse inside each flower, then fold over the petals to close it up. Heat the oil in a deep pan. Stir the batter, dip in the flowers a few at a time, and fry in the hot oil for a minute or two until golden and crisp. Drain on kitchen paper and serve at once.

Cucumber Mousse

SERVES 6

A delicate summer mousse. If preferred, the mousse can be set in individual ramekins.

1 cucumber, peeled and halved
salt
1 tablespoon water
1 tablespoon white wine vinegar
½ oz (15 g) powdered gelatine
⅛ pint (75 ml) good chicken stock
4 oz (100 g) cream cheese
juice of ½ small lemon
⅛ pint (75 ml) mayonnaise (page 67)
¼ pint (150 ml) whipping cream, whipped
freshly ground black pepper
2 teaspoons snipped chives
1 bunch watercress, trimmed, for garnish
slices of cucumber, for garnish

USING THE FINE
SLICING DISC:
METAL BLADE

Cut one half of the cucumber into fairly small dice, spread them out on a plate and sprinkle with salt. Slice the remaining cucumber in the processor, arrange the slices on another plate and sprinkle with salt. Set both plates of cucumber aside for the salt to draw out excess water – this will take about an hour. Rinse the cucumber dice and slices separately with cold water, drain and pat dry.

Measure the water and the vinegar into a small bowl and sprinkle on the gelatine. Leave it for a few minutes to swell. Stand the bowl in a pan of simmering water until the gelatine has dissolved. Allow it to cool a little, then stir it into the stock.

Fit the metal blade. Put the cheese in the processor bowl and process briefly, then add the sliced cucumber, lemon juice and mayonnaise and process until the cucumber is puréed. Scrape down the sides of the bowl, add the whipped cream, pepper, snipped chives and stock and process again until well mixed. Finally, add the diced cucumber and process only very briefly – just enough to mix in the cucumber but not enough to chop the dice. Taste the mixture and check seasoning, then pour into a lightly greased 1½ pint (900 ml) ring mould or shallow dish. Chill until set.

To serve, dip the mould into a bowl of very hot water for a moment, put a damp plate on top and invert the mould to turn out the mousse. Fill the centre of the mousse with trimmed watercress and garnish with cucumber slices.

Soups

*P*uréed soups are wonderful, but with a processor you can actually make soups with a variety of textures. All that's needed is a little precision and care when cooking and processing. Be careful not to cook vegetables too long before processing as they will lose both colour and flavour. It is a shame to end up with a grey/green spinach soup just because you've overcooked the spinach.

Make soups from ingredients that you have in the garden or refrigerator. Use fresh raw vegetables or lightly cooked leftover vegetables and vary the ingredients according to the time of year. In late summer use fresh tomatoes instead of canned, and use leeks when they are plentiful, instead of onions, to make a change.

You can make puréed vegetable soups without any added thickening or you can include leftover cooked rice or pasta before processing to give a soup extra body. Rice can also be dropped into soups for texture.

Leftovers from a good casserole can be transformed into wonderful meat soups in the processor. Add extra stock and vegetables if necessary.

Watercress Soup

◆

SERVES 6

For this soup you can use watercress that is just past its best and needs using up, or use landcress if you grow it. This is also good served chilled but may need thinning with a little milk or stock.

1 large onion, cut into quarters
12 oz (350 g) potatoes, peeled
2 oz (50 g) butter
1 pint (600 ml) good chicken stock
salt
freshly ground black pepper
2 bunches watercress, washed but not trimmed
¾ pint (450 ml) milk
¼ pint (150 ml) single cream

USING THE FINE
SLICING DISC:
METAL BLADE

Slice the onion and potatoes in the processor.

Melt the butter in a pan and gently cook the onion and potato for about 5 minutes. Do not allow them to brown.

Add the stock and seasoning to the pan and bring to the boil, then cover and simmer for about 15 minutes. Add the watercress and simmer for a further 10 minutes.

Fit the metal blade. Empty the saucepan into the processor bowl and process the mixture until really smooth. Rinse out the saucepan, then pour the purée into the pan, stir in the milk and heat through. Taste and check seasoning. Stir in the cream to serve.

Cucumber and Mint Soup

◆

SERVES 6

A wonderful summer soup, good either hot or well chilled.

2 large cucumbers, peeled and seeded
1 medium-sized onion
2 oz (50 g) butter
1½ oz (40 g) flour
1 pint (600 ml) good chicken stock
9 sprigs fresh mint
½ pint (300 ml) milk
single cream, to serve

USING THE FINE
SLICING DISC:
METAL BLADE

Cut half of one of the cucumbers into neat dice and set aside. Slice the remaining cucumber and the onion in the processor. Melt the butter in a large saucepan, add the sliced cucumber and onion and sauté, covered, for about 15 minutes.

Sprinkle on the flour and cook for a minute more, stirring, then gradually blend in the stock and bring to the boil, stirring until thickened. Add 6 of the mint sprigs, season and simmer very gently for about 10 minutes. Remove the mint.

Fit the metal blade. Empty the saucepan into the processor bowl and process the mixture to a fine purée.

Rinse out the saucepan, then pour the soup into the pan. Stir in the milk and diced cucumber and heat until piping hot. Taste and season, adding more milk if you prefer a thinner soup.

Chop the leaves from the remaining mint sprigs in the processor, and serve the soup with a swirl of cream and a sprinkling of chopped mint.

Carrot and Orange Soup

SERVES 8

One of our favourite soups. If preferred, use a 1 pint (600 ml) carton of fresh orange juice and less stock.

>2 lb (900 g) carrots
>2 lb (900 g) onions
>1 oz (25 g) butter
>1 tablespoon sunflower oil
>3 pints (1.75 litres) good light stock
>salt
>freshly ground black pepper
>6 oz (175 g) carton concentrated frozen orange juice
>small bunch of parsley, for garnish

USING THE COARSE
SLICING DISC:
METAL BLADE

Slice the carrots and onions in the processor. Heat the butter and oil in a large pan and sauté the carrots and onions with the lid on for about 10 minutes.

Pour the stock into the pan, season and bring to the boil. Cover and simmer for about 30 minutes, until the vegetables are just tender.

Fit the metal blade and purée the soup in the processor. Rinse out the pan, then return the soup to the pan. Stir in the orange juice and reheat until piping hot. Taste and check seasoning.

Chop the parsley in the processor and sprinkle over the soup to serve.

Vichyssoise

SERVES 6

Classic leek and potato soup. Traditionally served chilled but well worth trying hot for a change.

12 oz (350 g) leeks, cleaned
12 oz (350 g) potatoes, peeled
2 oz (50 g) butter
1 oz (25 g) flour
1 pint (600 ml) good chicken stock
salt
freshly ground black pepper
½ pint (300 ml) milk
a little single cream
snipped chives, for garnish

USING THE COARSE
SLICING DISC:
METAL BLADE

Slice the leeks and potatoes in the processor, keeping them separate. Melt the butter in a large saucepan, add the leeks and fry gently for about 5 minutes without browning.

Stir in the flour, then gradually blend in the stock, stirring. Add the potatoes to the pan, season with salt and pepper, stir in the milk and bring to the boil. Simmer for about 30 minutes, until the vegetables are tender.

Fit the metal blade and purée the soup, in two batches if necessary. Taste and check seasoning.

Chill well, then thin if necessary with milk or stock before serving. Garnish with a swirl of cream and some snipped chives. To serve hot, reheat gently and add a little cream to each bowl of soup.

French Onion Soup

SERVES 8–10

Served with a slice of French bread topped with melted grated cheese floating on each bowl, this makes a substantial soup or light lunch.

2 lb (900 g) Spanish onions, cut into quarters
4 tablespoons sunflower oil
1½ oz (40 g) butter
1 tablespoon sugar
2 oz (50 g) flour
3 pints (1.75 litres) good beef stock
salt
freshly ground black pepper
4 oz (100 g) Cheddar cheese
8–10 slices French bread, ½ inch (1.25 cm) thick

USING THE COARSE SLICING DISC: FINE GRATING DISC

Slice the onions in the processor. Heat the oil and butter in a large pan, then add the onions and fry gently to soften. Add the sugar when the onions are soft, to help them brown.

When the onions are a good colour, stir in the flour and cook for a minute or two. Gradually add the stock and bring to the boil, stirring all the time. Add the seasoning, cover with a lid and simmer for 30–40 minutes.

Meanwhile, fit the grating disc and grate the cheese in the processor. Toast the French bread slices on one side under the grill. Sprinkle the grated cheese over the untoasted side of the bread. When ready to serve, melt and brown the cheese under a hot grill.

Taste the soup and check seasoning. Float one slice of toasted French bread and cheese on each bowl of soup.

Gazpacho

SERVES 6

This is one of the quickest of all soups to make in the processor and a good soup to make in the late summer when tomatoes are at their cheapest and best. If they're expensive, use two 14 oz (400 g) cans of chopped tomatoes instead. If you have a small processor you may have to process the ingredients in several batches.

1 large Spanish onion, cut into quarters
2 lb (900 g) ripe tomatoes, skinned and quartered
2 fat cloves garlic, crushed
4 tablespoons white wine vinegar
5 tablespoons olive oil
1/2 pint (300 ml) good chicken stock
2 oz (50 g) green pepper, finely diced
juice of 1/2 lemon
salt
freshly ground black pepper
diced cucumber and small bread croûtons, for garnish

USING THE METAL BLADE

Process the onion finely. Add the tomatoes and process again. Add the garlic, vinegar, oil and stock and process until smooth and well blended.

Turn the mixture into a bowl and stir in the green pepper dice, lemon juice and seasoning. Chill for at least 6 hours.

Serve icy cold, garnished with diced cucumber and croûtons.

Healthy Vegetable Soup

SERVES 6

No flour is added to the soup and very little oil is used, so this is a delicious meal with few calories.

1 lb (450 g) onions
2 medium-sized carrots
1 lb (450 g) potatoes, peeled
2 tablespoons sunflower oil
1 tablespoon paprika
14 oz (400 g) can peeled tomatoes
2 pints (1.2 litres) good beef stock
salt and freshly ground black pepper
bunch of parsley, for garnish

USING THE COARSE GRATING DISC: METAL BLADE

Grate the onions, carrots and potatoes in the processor. Heat the oil in a large pan, add the vegetables, cover and sauté for about 10 minutes.

Stir in the paprika and cook for a few moments, then pour in the tomatoes and stock. Bring to the boil, cover and simmer for about 30 minutes, until the vegetables are tender.

Meanwhile, fit the metal blade and chop the parsley. Taste the soup and check seasoning, then serve piping hot, sprinkled with parsley.

Curried Apple Soup

SERVES 6

Something different, and delicious either hot or cold.

> 1 onion, cut into quarters
> 1 oz (25 g) butter
> 1½ teaspoons ground coriander
> 1 teaspoon ground cummin
> 1 teaspoon ground turmeric
> 1½ teaspoons garam masala
> 1½ oz (40 g) flour
> 1½ pints (900 ml) water
> 2 chicken stock cubes
> 1½ lb (675 g) cooking apples, peeled and roughly chopped
> salt
> freshly ground black pepper
> 2 tablespoons mango chutney
> juice of ½ lemon
> ¼ pint (150 ml) natural yoghurt

USING THE METAL BLADE

Process the onion until roughly chopped. Melt the butter in a large pan, add the onion and fry slowly, covered, for 5 minutes or until soft.

Stir the spices into the onion and cook for a further minute, then add the flour and cook for another minute. Add the water, stock cubes, apples and seasoning, bring to the boil, stirring, and simmer for 15 minutes. Allow to cool a little.

Stir in the mango chutney and lemon juice, then process the soup, in two or three batches, until smooth.

Rinse out the saucepan, pour the soup into the pan and bring to the boil. Taste and check seasoning and consistency.

Add a spoonful of yoghurt to each bowl of soup to serve.

If serving cold, taste and check seasoning and thin the soup with a little more stock or water as necessary.

Dutch Split Pea Soup

SERVES 6–8

Inexpensive and easy to make, this is a delicious winter soup and can be served with garlic croûtons or thinly sliced frankfurter sausages. If you have a good heavy preserving pan make double the quantity – it freezes well.

> *1 gammon knuckle or 2 pig's trotters*
> *1 lb (450 g) green or yellow split peas*
> *4 pints (2.25 litres) water*
> *4 sticks celery*
> *12 oz (350 g) potatoes*
> *2 leeks*
> *8 oz (225 g) onions, quartered*
> *salt*
> *freshly ground black pepper*

USING THE COARSE SLICING DISC: METAL BLADE

Soak the gammon or pig's trotters overnight in enough cold water to cover. Drain and put into a generous-sized pan with the water and the peas. Simmer uncovered for an hour.

Slice the celery, potatoes and leeks in the processor. Fit the metal blade and coarsely chop the onions. Add the vegetables to the pan, cover and continue to simmer for 1½–2½ hours, or until the split peas are cooked.

Remove the gammon or pig's trotters and strain the soup into a large bowl. Process the peas and vegetables in two lots, adding some of the strained liquid through the funnel. Combine with the rest of the liquid and season to taste. Bring the soup back to the boil before serving.

If you like, take any meat off the gammon knuckle or trotters and serve it in the soup.

Fish

◆

*T*his section is small as I think that generally fish is best left whole or in fillets or cutlets, rather than chopped or puréed. The exceptions are quenelles and fish cakes.

I use the processor for chopping herbs to add to sauces to go with fish, for making light stuffings and toppings and to purée vegetables such as spinach, sorrel or celeriac (page 59) to serve as an accompaniment. If you are coating fish in egg and fresh bread-crumbs, chop some parsley in the processor and add it to the crumbs – which can also be made in the processor. You can also mix up a quick batter in the processor if you are having deep-fried fish.

Baked Fish with Wholewheat and Cheese Topping

SERVES 4

This recipe was given to me by my cousin who lives in Holland. The crunchy topping is a mixture of cheese and breadcrumbs.

1 lb (450 g) cod fillet, or other white fish
juice of 1 lemon
¼ pint (150 ml) cider or white wine
salt
freshly ground black pepper
1 onion, cut into quarters
2 oz (50 g) butter
1½ oz (40 g) flour
½ pint (300 ml) milk
4 oz (100 g) peeled prawns
small bunch of parsley
2 oz (50 g) wholemeal bread
2 oz (50 g) Cheddar cheese

USING THE METAL
BLADE: COARSE
GRATING DISC

Put the fish in a shallow pan, pour over the lemon juice and cider or wine and season with salt and pepper. Cover with a lid and poach gently for 10–15 minutes, until the fish is cooked.

Remove from the heat, lift the fish out of the pan and pour the cooking juices into a jug. Roughly flake the fish and discard any skin and bones.

Process the onion for a few moments until quite coarsely chopped. Heat the butter in a saucepan and fry the onion gently for about 10 minutes, until softened.

Stir the flour into the onions and cook for a moment, then gradually blend in the milk. Bring to the boil, stirring until thickened. Blend in the cooking juices from the fish and bring back to the boil. Remove from the heat and stir in the flaked fish and prawns.

Heat the oven to 400°F/200°C/gas mark 6. Roughly chop the parsley in the processor and stir into sauce. Taste and check seasoning, then turn into a shallow ovenproof dish.

Break the bread into pieces, then process until fine crumbs. Fit the coarse grating disc and grate the cheese. Mix together lightly and spoon over the fish. Bake in the oven for about 20 minutes and serve piping hot.

FACING PAGE, TOP: *Thatched Mashed Potatoes (page 62)*, BELOW: *Stuffed Green Peppers (page 52)*

Quenelles with Asparagus Sauce

◆

SERVES 4–6

A light fish recipe quickly prepared using the processor. The quenelles can be made and poached ahead of time. To reheat, arrange in an ovenproof dish, cover with foil and heat through at 300°F/150°C/gas mark 2 for about 40 minutes. Make the sauce just before serving.

1 lb (450 g) cod fillet, skinned, boned and roughly cut up
2 egg whites
salt
freshly ground black pepper
¼ pint (150 ml) double cream

ASPARAGUS SAUCE
6 tablespoons white wine
8 oz (225 g) fresh or frozen asparagus
½ pint (300 ml) double cream
salt
freshly ground black pepper

USING THE METAL BLADE

Put the cod, egg whites and seasoning in the processor bowl and process until absolutely smooth. With the machine still running, add the cream in a steady stream until thoroughly blended. Do not overprocess as the cream can curdle. Turn into a bowl, cover and chill for several hours.

To cook the quenelles, simmer a large pan of salted water. Dip a dessertspoon in the hot water, then take a generous spoonful of the chilled mixture, smooth the top with another spoon and lower it into the water. Tap the spoon gently on the bottom of the pan and the quenelle will come away from the spoon. Poach the quenelles about six at a time for 6–10 minutes in simmering water, then lift out carefully using a slotted spoon. Arrange in an ovenproof dish and keep warm.

For the sauce, measure the wine into a small pan and boil rapidly until reduced to a thin syrup. Meanwhile cook the asparagus in boiling salted water until tender, then drain. Cut off the tips and reserve for garnish. They can be kept warm with the quenelles. Put the reduced wine and asparagus stems in the processor bowl and process until quite smooth.

Pour the cream into the pan used for the wine, bring to the boil and cook until it will coat the back of a metal spoon. Stir in the asparagus purée and season to taste.

Arrange the quenelles on serving plates. Pour the sauce over and around them and garnish each plate with asparagus spears.

FACING PAGE: *Quenelles with Asparagus Sauce (above)*

Fishcakes

SERVES 16–20

I always make a lot of fishcakes at a time in the vain hope that I will have plenty left to freeze! Freeze them before frying.

6 oz (175 g) fresh bread
good bunch of parsley
2 lb (900 g) potatoes, peeled and boiled
2 oz (50 g) butter
2 lb (900 g) white fish, cooked and flaked
salt
freshly ground black pepper
anchovy essence (optional)
1 egg
a little sunflower oil

USING THE METAL BLADE

Process the bread to fine crumbs and set aside. Process the parsley and put it in a large mixing bowl. Mash the potatoes with the butter, turn into the bowl with the parsley and add the flaked fish, salt, pepper and anchovy essence, if using.

With your hands, shape the mixture into 16–20 flat cakes. Break the egg into a deep plate and whisk with a fork, adding a little water. Turn the fish cakes over in the egg, then coat with the breadcrumbs.

Heat a spoonful of sunflower oil in a heavy frying pan. Fry the fish cakes a few at a time for about 5 minutes on each side.

Trout with Hazelnuts and Kiwi Fruit

SERVES 4

Farmed trout are available fresh in most supermarkets. Buy them filleted and allow one fillet per person. Hazelnuts and kiwi fruit go well together and are particularly nice with trout.

4 trout fillets
2 oz (50 g) shelled hazelnuts
2 oz (50 g) brown bread
melted butter
2 kiwi fruit
salt
freshly ground black pepper

USING THE METAL
BLADE

Heat the oven to 350°F/180°C/gas mark 4. Butter a baking tray and lay the trout fillets on it skin side down.

Process the hazelnuts, then add the bread and seasoning to the processor and process so the bread is reduced to crumbs and mixed with the nuts in one operation.

Brush the fish fillets with melted butter and cover them evenly with the crumb and nut mixture. Bake in the oven for about 20 minutes. The fish should be cooked but still nicely moist.

Peel the kiwi fruit and slice them thinly, using a sharp knife. Lay overlapping slices on each trout fillet to serve.

Stuffed Lemon Soles

SERVES 4

Any medium-sized flat fish can be used instead of sole.

4 oz (100 g) button mushrooms
1½ oz (40 g) butter
3 oz (75 g) fresh bread
4 spring onions
good bunch of parsley
grated rind and juice of 1 lemon
salt
freshly ground black pepper
4 whole lemon soles, about 12 oz (350 g) each

USING THE FINE
SLICING DISC:
METAL BLADE

Begin by preparing the stuffing. Slice the mushrooms in the processor. Melt the butter in a pan, add the mushrooms and soften gently, then transfer to a medium-sized bowl.

Fit the metal blade. Put the bread in the processor bowl and process into crumbs, then add the spring onions and parsley and process to chop. Add the mixture to the mushrooms with the lemon rind, juice and seasoning and mix well together.

Clean the fish and remove their heads. Trim the fins and tails with sharp scissors. Place each fish, dark side down, on a board and with a sharp knife make a cut through the white skin along the backbone to within ⅝ inch (1.5 cm) of each end. Ease the flesh away from either side of the bone to form two pockets, then fill the pockets with stuffing.

Heat the oven to 400°F/200°C/gas mark 6 and butter a shallow oven-proof dish. Lay fish in the dish, dot with a little butter, cover with foil and cook in the oven for about 20 minutes, until just tender. To serve, lift each fish on to a warmed serving plate.

Main Courses

Main courses in the 1990s don't necessarily mean meat and two veg. There are all sorts of other interesting things you can include in a main course – Fresh Vegetables with Pesto (page 55), Stuffed Green Peppers (page 52) or Vicarage Nut Roast (page 49), to name but a few – and the processor can help you make them all quickly and easily. And with more traditional meals it may not be the meat that requires processing but the etceteras, such as a stuffing or the pastry to go over a meat pie.

But the processor is of course marvellous for mincing or chopping meat, and doing this yourself at home means you can choose the exact cut and leanness of meat to use. Another great advantage is that the processor will cut up meat to the degree of fineness that you want for a recipe. Keep a watchful eye on the machine, especially with raw meat, and check at frequent intervals.

The last rather tatty looking bits of the Sunday joint can be chopped or minced in the processor and made just as delicious the second time around – Mansion Pie (page 40) is piquant and a top favourite with us. Leftover meat also makes a versatile stuffing for aubergines or marrow (page 42) and pancakes.

Mediterranean Stuffed Beef Rolls

SERVES 4

Thin slices of beef rolled around a very fresh, light stuffing of seasonal vegetables make a healthy low-fat main course.

2 sticks celery
1 carrot, peeled and cut in half
4 oz (100 g) mushrooms
1 red pepper, seeded and cut into quarters
1 medium-sized onion, cut into quarters
knob of butter
4 thin slices of topside of beef, about 1¼ lb (550 g) total weight
salt
freshly ground black pepper
½ pint (300 ml) good beef stock
¼ pint (150 ml) natural yoghurt
chopped parsley, to serve

USING THE FINE SLICING DISC

Slice the vegetables in the processor and put them in a large frying pan with the butter. Stir and fry them quickly so that they soften slightly but still retain texture and colour. Leave to cool.

Heat the oven to 400°F/200°C/gas mark 6. Lay a slice of beef between two pieces of greaseproof paper and use a rolling pin to flatten and enlarge the meat, then cut it in two. Repeat with the other three slices.

Divide the vegetable mixture among the eight pieces of beef, putting it to one end so you can roll them up. Secure with wooden cocktail sticks, then pack the rolls into an ovenproof dish. Season with salt and pepper, then pour on the stock so it comes about half way up the rolls and cook in the oven for ¾–1 hour, until the meat is tender.

Take the meat dish out of the oven and lift out the rolls one at a time, removing the cocktail sticks. Arrange the rolls on a serving dish.

Pour the cooking liquor into a saucepan and reduce over a high heat to about ¼ pint (150 ml). Allow to cool a little and mix in the yoghurt. Taste and check seasoning. Heat gently without boiling, then pour over the beef rolls. Sprinkle with chopped parsley and serve immediately.

American Beefburgers

SERVES 4

Home-made beefburgers are better than any bought ones if you use prime qualify beef. They are not always cheaper, but they do contain much more meat, and far less fat. These are particularly delicious when cooked on the barbecue.

1 small onion
1½ lb (675 g) chuck steak, cut into large pieces
salt
freshly ground black pepper
a little flour
a little oil, for frying

USING THE COARSE
GRATING DISC:
METAL BLADE

Grate the onion in the processor and put to one side in a large bowl.

Fit the metal blade and finely mince the meat, then add it to the onion with the seasoning and mix well together. Divide the mixture into four large or eight small portions and shape into beefburgers on a floured surface.

Fry in oil until nicely brown (about 4 minutes on each side) or cook on the barbecue, greasing the racks well first.

Serve hot with Fresh Tomato Sauce (page 72) or Barbecue Sauce (page 70).

Corned Beef Hash

SERVES 6

Americans crave for hash! It makes a different lunch in the school holidays, when you're running out of ideas.

1 medium-sized onion, cut in half
2½ oz (60 g) butter
2 lb (900 g) potatoes, peeled
12 oz (350 g) can corned beef
a little milk
salt
freshly ground black pepper
1 tablespoon sunflower oil

USING THE FINE
SLICING DISC:
COARSE GRATING
DISC

Slice the onion in the processor. Melt 1 oz (25 g) of the butter in a pan, add the onion and soften over a low heat for 5 minutes.

Fit the coarse grating disc. Grate the potatoes, then blanch for 2 minutes in plenty of boiling salted water. Drain and turn into a generous-sized bowl. Add the onion and corned beef, mix together with milk to form a spreading consistency and season to taste.

Heat the remaining butter and the oil in a large frying pan. Spread the hash evenly in the pan and cook slowly until browned on the bottom – about 40 minutes. Put the pan under a hot grill. When the top is crispy, slide on to a hot plate and serve.

Frikadeller

◆

SERVES 6–8

These delicious Danish meatballs should be served hot with Fresh Tomato Sauce (page 72). If you are already using a hot oven, preheat the fat in a roasting tin and cook the meatballs for 15–20 minutes, turning once, instead of frying them.

1 large onion
1 oz (25 g) butter
2 tablespoons sunflower oil
1 lb (450 g) pork, cut into chunks
1 lb (450 g) beef, cut into chunks
4 oz (100 g) fresh wholemeal bread, broken in pieces
2 eggs
3 fl oz (90 ml) milk
salt
freshly ground black pepper

USING THE METAL
BLADE

Put the onion in the processor bowl and process until finely chopped. Melt the butter and 1 tablespoon of oil in a pan and fry the onion for about 10 minutes, until golden brown. Turn into a large mixing bowl.

Process the meats in two batches until finely chopped, being careful not to overprocess. Add the bread and process until it forms fairly fine crumbs, then tip the meat and breadcrumbs into the bowl with the onion. Lastly, add the eggs and milk to the bowl and stir thoroughly. Season well and mix again thoroughly. Cover with clear film and chill in the refrigerator until really cold – several hours, or preferably overnight.

To shape into frikadeller, take 2 dessertspoons of the meat mixture and form into an egg shape. Return the meatballs to the refrigerator for about 2 hours before cooking.

Heat the remaining oil in a large pan and fry the frikadeller gently for about 15 minutes, until golden brown all over.

Mansion Pie

SERVES 6

Posh Cottage Pie! For everyday you can leave out the port and green pepper, but remember to increase the stock if you omit the port.

3 tablespoons oil
6 oz (175 g) button mushrooms, cut into quarters
1 large onion, cut into eight pieces
1 green pepper, seeded
1 fat clove garlic, crushed
about 1 lb (450 g) cooked beef or lamb
a generous tablespoon of flour
14 oz (400 g) can chopped tomatoes
scant ½ pint (300 ml) stock
1 tablespoon Worcestershire sauce
4 tablespoons port
sprig of thyme
bay leaf
salt
freshly ground black pepper

TOPPING
2 lb (900 g) potatoes, peeled
a little milk
knob of butter
salt
freshly ground black pepper
2 oz (50 g) mature Cheddar cheese

USING THE METAL BLADE: COARSE GRATING DISC

Measure the oil into a large pan, add the mushrooms and cook quickly for a few moments. Lift out and keep on one side.

Chop the onion in the processor, then the green pepper. Add to the pan with the garlic and a little more oil if necessary, and fry quickly for 5 minutes.

Process the meat until finely chopped and add to the pan. Cook for a few minutes, then sprinkle in the flour and add the tomatoes, stock, Worcestershire sauce, port, thyme and bay leaf. Season well, bring to the boil and simmer for about 15 minutes. Remove the thyme and bay leaf and check seasoning. Add the mushrooms and turn into a shallow 2½ pint (1.5 litre) pie dish. Leave to cool.

Boil the potatoes for the topping and mash them with butter and milk, then season and spread over the meat. Heat the oven to 425°F/220°C/gas mark 7.

Fit the grating disc. Grate the cheese in the processor, sprinkle on top of the potato and cook the pie in the oven for 20–25 minutes, until brown, hot and bubbling.

Stuffed Vine Leaves

◆

SERVES 4–6

Packets of preserved vine leaves are available in supermarkets if you don't have access to fresh ones, and if unopened will keep for quite a time.

Stuffed vine leaves make an unusual main course or are just as nice served cold as a first course.

1 onion, cut into quarters
1 lb (450 g) lean leg or fillet of lamb, cut into chunks
2 oz (50 g) cooked long-grain rice
1 oz (25 g) raisins
salt
freshly ground black pepper
1/4 pint (150 ml) white wine or stock
about 20 fresh vine leaves, blanched, or 1 packet preserved vine
*   leaves, rinsed and drained*
2 tablespoons chopped fresh mint
scant 1/4 pint (150 ml) olive oil
1/4 pint (150 ml) natural yoghurt

USING THE METAL BLADE

Chop the onion finely in the processor and set aside. Process the meat until finely minced, then put the onion and meat in a frying pan and fry gently for about 5 minutes so that the fat runs out. Stir in the rice, raisins, seasoning and wine and simmer for about 10 minutes. Leave to cool.

Heat the oven to 350°F/180°C/gas mark 4 and lightly oil a shallow ovenproof dish. Sort through the vine leaves and snip off any tough stalks. Any torn leaves can be used to line the dish.

Stir the mint into the meat mixture. Place a spoonful of the mixture on each vine leaf, fold in the sides and roll up like a parcel. Place the parcels close together in the dish. Keeping them closely packed prevents them from coming undone and they retain a nice compact shape. When all the mixture is used up, pour over the oil and cover with spare leaves or foil. Cook for about 45 minutes.

Remove the top leaves or foil and pour over the yoghurt. Return the dish to the oven to heat the yoghurt through. Serve hot.

Roast Stuffed Aubergines

SERVES 4

These freeze very well, before their final browning in the oven, and are another tasty way of using up leftover cooked meat.

2 large onions
2 aubergines, leaf bases trimmed
olive oil
8 oz (225 g) cooked lamb or beef
14 oz (400 g) can chopped tomatoes
2 cloves garlic, crushed
sprig of thyme
salt
freshly ground black pepper
2 oz (50 g) fresh bread
a little well-flavoured Cheddar cheese

USING THE METAL
BLADE: COARSE
GRATING DISC

Heat the oven to 350°F/180°C/gas mark 4 and grease an ovenproof dish. Chop the onion in the processor, put it in a pan of boiling water with the aubergines and boil for about 5 minutes. Drain the aubergines and onions. Plunge the aubergines into cold water and leave for about 5 minutes. Cut in half lengthwise and scoop out the flesh, leaving a ½ inch (1.25 cm) thick shell. Set the flesh aside.

Arrange the aubergine shells in the ovenproof dish, season and pour 4 teaspoons of oil into each shell. Roast in the oven for about 15 minutes.

Finely mince the meat in the processor. Transfer to a frying pan with a little oil and fry for about 5 minutes. Chop the aubergine flesh in the processor, but not too finely, then add to the meat and fry for a few minutes. Add the tomatoes, onions, garlic and leaves from the sprig of thyme. Cook until most of the tomato juice has been absorbed and the meat is tender. Season to taste and use to fill the roasted aubergine shells.

Process the bread slices to make breadcrumbs, then fit the grating disc and grate the cheese. Mix the bread and cheese together and sprinkle on top of the aubergines. Bake in the oven for about 20 minutes, until the topping is golden.

Variation

Stuffed Marrow

Peel the marrow, then cut it into thick slices and remove the seeds. Blanch the slices in boiling water for 5 minutes and drain well. Lay the slices on a greased baking sheet. Fill the centres with the stuffing mixture (just omit the aubergine flesh), top with cheese and breadcrumbs and bake as above.

English Lamb Stuffed with Watercress and Ham

SERVES 8

The leg bone is removed from the lamb and in its place are put rolls of ham spread with a stuffing made from watercress, breadcrumbs and garlic.

1 medium leg of English lamb
1 bunch watercress, washed and trimmed
2 oz (50 g) brown bread
2 fat cloves garlic, crushed
4 slices ham
salt
freshly ground black pepper
2 large onions, cut into quarters
1 glass white wine

USING THE METAL BLADE: FINE OR COARSE SLICING DISC

Using a sharp knife, bone the lamb, leaving the shank bone in place (or get your butcher to do this for you). Heat the oven to 350°F/180°C/gas mark 4.

Finely chop the watercress in the processor. Add the bread and reduce to fine crumbs, then mix the crushed garlic into the watercress and breadcrumbs. Spread the ham slices with the watercress and crumb mixture. Season, then roll up the slices and stuff them into the lamb where the bone has been removed. Any leftover stuffing mixture can be put around the ham rolls.

Fit the slicing disc and slice the onions. Place them in a large casserole and lay the lamb on top. Pour over the wine and season with salt and black pepper. Cover with a lid or foil and cook for 35 minutes per pound (450 g) plus an extra 35 minutes. After an hour reduce the oven temperature to 325°F/170°C/gas mark 3 and continue cooking without covering. If you like lamb to be pink reduce the cooking time to 20 minutes per pound (450 g) plus an extra 20 minutes.

Chicken and Cashew Nut Stir-Fry

SERVES 4

Stir-frying is a quick and healthy way of cooking. Vegetables are lightly cooked to retain their crispness and vitamins. It helps to freeze the chicken breasts for 2 hours to firm up the flesh before cutting into strips.

2 chicken breasts, skinned and boned
2 or 3 celery sticks
1 small red pepper
4 spring onions
4 oz (100 g) button mushrooms
2 tablespoons oil
4 oz (100 g) small mange-tout, strings removed
4 oz (100 g) bean sprouts
2 oz (50 g) salted cashew nuts
soy sauce

USING THE FINE
SLICING DISC

Cut each of the chicken breasts into pencil-thin strips using a sharp knife. Finely slice the celery, red pepper, spring onions and mushrooms in the processor.

Measure the oil into a wok or large frying pan and fry the chicken strips on maximum heat for 2 minutes, until nicely brown. Add all the vegetables except the bean sprouts and stir-fry briefly – the vegetables should still have crispness.

Lastly, add the bean sprouts, cashew nuts and soy sauce. Heat through until bubbling and serve at once.

Chicken Paupiettes

SERVES 6

These are delicious and simple to make. Flattened breasts of chicken are rolled around a chestnut and bacon stuffing and served with a lemon cream sauce. The chicken and stuffing can be prepared ahead so that there is no last minute panic in the kitchen before a dinner party. The sauce can be made in advance, too, but don't add the tarragon until you are almost ready to serve. Then reheat the sauce over a pan of simmering water.

6 chicken breasts, skinned and boned
salt
freshly ground black pepper
juice of ½ lemon

STUFFING
2 oz (50 g) streaky bacon
1 small onion, cut into quarters
scant tablespoon olive oil
3 oz (75 g) canned or frozen peeled chestnuts, lightly chopped
2 oz (50 g) bread, broken in pieces
1 egg

SAUCE
3 oz (75 g) butter, melted
juice of 1 lemon
½ teaspoon flour
½ pint (300 ml) single cream
1 egg yolk
a few sprigs of tarragon

USING THE METAL
BLADE

First make the stuffing. Cut the bacon into pieces and process finely. Using a non-stick frying pan, cook over a low heat until the fat begins to run. Process the onions briefly and add to the bacon, then cover the pan and fry for about 10 minutes. Add the oil if necessary, according to how fatty the bacon is. Add the chestnuts and cook slowly for a further 10 minutes.

Put the bread in the processor bowl and process briefly to make crumbs. Put into a fairly large mixing bowl and add the bacon mixture and the egg. Season lightly and mix well.

Heat the oven to 375°F/190°C/gas mark 5. Spread the chicken breasts out on a layer of clear film, cover with a second layer and beat out gently with a rolling pin. Remove the clear film and season lightly with salt, pepper and lemon juice. Divide the stuffing into six and spread down the middle of each chicken breast. Roll up and place close together in an ovenproof dish. Cover loosely with foil and cook in the oven for 30–40 minutes, according to the size of the chicken breasts.

To make the sauce, put all the ingredients except the tarragon into the processor bowl and process until smooth. Transfer to a double saucepan or a heatproof bowl set over a pan of boiling water, and stir occasionally until thick. Put the tarragon into a clean processor bowl and process briefly, then add to the sauce and season to taste.

Arrange the paupiettes on a serving plate and serve with the sauce.

Filo Cases with Chicken and Vegetable Stir-Fry

◆

SERVES 4

Filo pastry is available frozen at most good supermarkets. Make the filo cases in advance and just reheat them before cooking the vegetables. Watch the cases carefully while in the oven – they can catch.

½ packet filo pastry, thawed
4 oz (100 g) butter, melted
4 sticks celery
8 oz (225 g) white cabbage
1 red pepper, seeded
1 green pepper, seeded
6 spring onions
3 skinless chicken breasts, cut into very fine slices
salt
freshly ground black pepper
olive oil

USING THE FINE SLICING DISC

Heat the oven to 350°F/180°C/gas mark 4 and have ready some greased or non-stick individual Yorkshire pudding tins.

Remove one sheet of pastry from the packet and cover the rest with a clean damp tea towel to prevent them from drying out. For each case cut four squares of pastry a bit larger than the moulds. Place one square in a mould and brush with melted butter. Place another square on the first one, but not exactly square to it, and brush again with melted butter. Do the same with the remaining two squares. There should now be little corners all around the edge. Repeat with the remaining pastry until you have about eight moulded cases. If you don't have enough tins, make the cases in batches. Bake in the oven for about 10 minutes, until golden brown. If necessary, remove from their tins and turn upside down to brown and crisp the base. Set aside until you are ready to reheat them to take the stir-fry.

Slice the vegetables in the processor, keeping each type separate.

Season the chicken with salt and pepper. Heat a tablespoon of oil in a wok or large frying pan and add the chicken, moving it about all the time until pale golden brown. Lift out with a slotted spoon, and keep warm. Put the pastry cases in a hot oven for about 5 minutes to heat through.

Measure another tablespoon of oil into the pan and add the sliced celery, cooking it briskly for about a minute. Add the white cabbage and cook for a minute or two, stirring all the time, then add the red and green peppers and finally the spring onions and seasoning. Return the chicken to the pan and mix. Spoon into the warm filo cases and serve.

Pheasant Normandy

SERVES 6–8

The cooking time of the pheasants will depend on their age. This recipe can be made ahead, cooled and kept in the refrigerator until needed, then reheated until very hot. The really good thing about this dish is that you have the basis, after carving, for a wonderful pheasant soup!

1 lb (450 g) cooking apples, peeled, cored and cut into quarters
1 onion, cut into quarters
2 oz (50 g) bacon
2 tablespoons oil
brace of pheasants
1 large clove garlic, crushed
good heaped tablespoon flour
¾ pint (450 ml) cider
salt
freshly ground black pepper
¼ pint (150 ml) double cream
chopped parsley, to serve

USING THE COARSE
SLICING DISC:
METAL BLADE

Heat oven to 350°F/180°C/gas mark 4. Slice the apples in the processor and set aside. Fit the metal blade. Chop the onion, then the bacon, and set aside.

Heat a tablespoon of oil in a large frying pan and fry the pheasants until lightly browned all over. Lift out and place in the bottom of a large ovenproof casserole. Fry the bacon, onion and garlic until brown and add to the casserole. Put the apple slices around the pheasants.

Heat the remaining tablespoon of oil and stir in the flour. Cook for a minute, then gradually add the cider, stirring continuously. When the sauce has come to the boil and thickened, season well and pour over the pheasants. Cover and cook for about 1½ hours, until the birds are tender.

Lift the pheasants out of the casserole and carve off the leg portions, then the breasts. (Use the wing ends and carcass for good game soup or stock, which can be frozen.) Pour the cooking liquor and apples into the processor bowl and purée until smooth, then add the cream and process again briefly.

Rinse out the casserole and return the meat to it. Taste the sauce, add more seasoning if necessary and pour over the meat. Serve with a sprinkling of chopped parsley.

Chicken and Watercress Raised Pie

SERVES 10

A good pie for a summer picnic. The crisp pastry is very quick to make in the processor and the layers of chicken contrast well in taste, texture and colour with the watercress filling.

FILLING
1 lb 4 oz (550 g) raw chicken breast
salt
freshly ground black pepper
2 tablespoons lemon juice
3 bunches of watercress, washed and dried
2 oz (50 g) shallots or spring onions, chopped
2 tablespoons flour
2 eggs
a little grated nutmeg
4 tablespoons double cream

PASTRY
12 oz (350 g) plain flour
salt
freshly ground black pepper
5 oz (150 g) lard
1/4 pint (150 ml) water
beaten egg, for glazing

USING THE METAL BLADE

First make the filling. Take one quarter of the chicken and cut it into thin slices using a sharp knife. Put to one side. Mince another quarter of the chicken in the processor, season with salt, pepper and lemon juice and briefly reprocess to mix. Put to one side. Cut the remaining chicken into chunks and put to one side.

Chop the watercress in the processor, add the chunks of chicken, the shallots, flour, eggs, nutmeg and seasoning and process finely. Add the cream and process briefly to mix.

Heat the oven to 425°F/220°C/gas mark 7. Measure the flour and seasoning for the pastry into the processor bowl. Place the lard and water in a pan and bring to the boil, making sure the lard has melted, then with the machine running pour in the water and lard through the funnel. Process until the dough is smooth and forms a ball. When cool enough to handle, take two thirds of the dough and mould it around the inside and up the sides of a 2 lb (900 g) tin.

Spoon half the watercress and chicken mixture into the bottom of the pie, lay the chicken slices carefully on top and cover with the plain processed chicken. Top with the remaining watercress and chicken mixture.

Knead the remaining pastry into an oblong about the size of the tin, lay it on top of the filling and press the edges firmly together. Trim the pastry, then flute the edges or just press with the prongs of a fork. Make four holes in the top of the pie and decorate with pastry letters or leaves, if liked. Brush with beaten egg and cook in the oven for 30 minutes, then reduce the heat to 350°F/180°C/gas mark 4 and cook for a further 30 minutes. Remove from the oven and leave to cool in the tin.

Chill the pie overnight before turning out. Serve whole on a plate, garnished with salad.

Vicarage Nut Roast

SERVES 4

Serve this hot with Vegetarian Gravy (page 73). It's equally good cold the next day with Fresh Tomato Sauce (page 72), if there is any left over.

1 large onion, cut into quarters
2 sticks celery, each cut into six pieces
1 egg, beaten
10 oz (275 g) unsalted mixed nuts, such as peanuts, walnuts, hazelnuts
3 oz (75 g) wholemeal bread
small bunch parsley
about ¼ pint (150 ml) vegetable stock
salt
freshly ground black pepper

USING THE METAL BLADE

Heat the oven to 375°F/190°C/gas mark 5 and grease a 1 lb (450 g) loaf tin.

Process the onion and celery for a few moments until coarsely chopped, then fry gently in a little oil until soft. Place in a large bowl with the egg.

Chop the nuts in the processor until they are as fine or coarse as you like them and add to the bowl. Process the bread into crumbs, then process the parsley, and add to the other ingredients. Add enough stock to moisten, season and mix together thoroughly.

Turn into the loaf tin and bake in the oven for about 30 minutes, or until golden brown. When cooled a little, turn out on to a serving plate and cut into slices to serve.

Spiced Nut Terrine

SERVES 6–8

This vegetarian terrine is easy to make and can be made a day in advance, so it is good for entertaining. Instead of a large terrine, you can cook the mixture in individual oval dishes for about 25 minutes. Serve with salad.

1 small onion, roughly cut
2 celery sticks, roughly cut
good knob of butter
1 teaspoon ground cummin
1 teaspoon dried mixed herbs
¼ pint (150 ml) red wine
6 oz (175 g) shelled walnuts
6 oz (175 g) blanched almonds
2 oz (50 g) brown bread
2 oz (50 g) fresh parsley
1 fat clove garlic, crushed
2 tablespoons soy sauce
2 tablespoons brandy
2 eggs
salt
freshly ground black pepper
sprigs of fresh herbs or thin slices of cucumber, for garnish

USING THE METAL BLADE

Heat the oven to 350°F/180°C/gas mark 4 and oil a 1½ pint (900 ml) oval terrine or tin.

Finely chop the onion and celery in the processor. Melt the butter in a saucepan, add the chopped vegetables and cook gently without colouring until soft. Add the cummin and mixed herbs and cook for about a minute. Pour in the wine and bring to the boil, stirring, then remove from the heat.

Measure the nuts, bread, parsley and garlic into the processor bowl and process until everything is finely chopped. Add the contents of the saucepan together with the soy sauce, brandy, eggs and plenty of seasoning. Process until well mixed.

Spoon the mixture into the terrine or tin, level the top and bake in the oven for about 40 minutes, until firm to the touch. Leave to cool, then refrigerate until ready to serve.

Turn out the terrine on to a plate. Decorate with sprigs of fresh herbs or thin slices of cucumber and serve in slices.

Florentine Pancakes

◆

SERVES 8

The filling may appear a little on the thick side at first, but it thins down when the spinach is added. Serve the pancakes piping hot with a crisp green salad and garlic bread. The pancakes may be frozen after rolling.

BATTER
4 oz (100 g) flour
1 egg
½ pint (300 ml) milk and water, mixed
1 tablespoon oil
oil for frying

FILLING
4 oz (100 g) Cheddar cheese
2 oz (50 g) butter
2 oz (50 g) flour
¾ pint (450 ml) milk
salt
freshly ground black pepper
1 teaspoon Dijon mustard
a little ground nutmeg
1 lb (450 g) frozen chopped leaf spinach, thawed and well
  drained
2 eggs, beaten

USING THE COARSE
GRATING DISC:
METAL BLADE

First grate the cheese for the filling. Set aside.

To make the pancakes, fit the metal blade and process the flour, eggs and half the milk and water until smooth. Scrape down the sides of the bowl, then, with the machine running, add the remaining milk and water and the oil through the funnel. Process until the batter is smooth.

Heat a little oil in an 8 inch (20 cm) frying pan. When it is hot, pour off the excess oil and add about 2 tablespoons of batter to the pan. Tip and rotate the pan so that the batter spreads evenly and covers the base thinly. Cook for about a minute until pale brown underneath, then turn over with a palette knife and cook for another minute. Slide the pancake out of the pan on to a plate. Make seven more pancakes.

Heat the oven to 350°F/180°C/gas mark 4. Melt the butter in a pan, stir in the flour and cook for a minute. Gradually blend in the milk and bring to the boil, stirring until thickened. Season well with salt, pepper, mustard and nutmeg. Stir in the spinach, eggs and 3 oz (75 g) of cheese. Allow to cool.

Divide the filling among the pancakes and roll up. Lay in an ovenproof dish, sprinkle with cheese and heat in the oven for about 25 minutes.

Stuffed Green Peppers

SERVES 4

Cook the rice until it is tender but still firm. The same filling can be used to stuff blanched rings of marrow or aubergines.

4 green peppers

STUFFING
1 medium onion
large knob of butter
4 oz (100 g) bacon, snipped
4 oz (100 g) mushrooms
4 oz (100 g) long grain brown rice, cooked
2 tablespoons chopped parsley
salt
freshly ground black pepper

CHEESE SAUCE
1½ oz (40 g) butter
1½ oz (40 g) flour
¾ pint (450 ml) milk
1 teaspoon Dijon mustard
grated nutmeg
salt
freshly ground black pepper
6 oz (175 g) well-flavoured Cheddar cheese
1 egg, beaten

USING THE METAL BLADE: COARSE SLICING DISC: COARSE GRATING DISC

Cut each pepper in half lengthwise, remove the stem and seeds and arrange the halves in a shallow ovenproof dish so that they fit snugly.

To make the stuffing, first chop the onion finely in the processor. Melt the butter in a large saucepan and fry the onion until soft, then add the bacon and cook for a few minutes more.

Fit the slicing disc and slice the mushrooms. Add them to the pan with the cooked rice, stirring well, then mix the parsley, into the stuffing. Season well and divide among the pepper halves.

For the cheese sauce, melt the butter in a pan, stir in the flour and cook for a minute. Gradually blend in the milk and bring to the boil, stirring until thickened. Remove from the heat, stir in the mustard and nutmeg and season well.

Heat the oven to 350°F/180°C/gas mark 4. Fit the grating disc and grate the cheese. Add about half the cheese to the sauce with the beaten egg and mix well together. Pour the sauce over and around the peppers. Sprinkle with the remaining cheese and bake in the oven for about an hour, until the peppers are tender.

Pizzas

◆

MAKES 2 LARGE
PIZZAS

Pepperoni is now available in supermarkets already sliced. It makes a wonderful hot spicy topping for pizzas. You can of course use home-made bread dough (pages 105 and 106) for the pizza bases instead of a packet mix – white and brown are equally good. You will need 8 oz (225 g) made weight of dough, risen once. If you make up a whole batch of dough, use some for the pizzas and some for rolls.

1 packet white bread mix
2 × recipe for Garlic Tomato Sauce (page 71)
small bunch of marjoram
4 oz (100 g) mozzarella cheese
4 oz (100 g) Cheddar cheese
1 green pepper, seeded
1 small onion
6 oz (175 g) pepperoni
a few black olives

USING THE METAL
BLADE: COARSE
GRATING DISC:
COARSE SLICING
DISC

Mix the dough base in the processor according to the instructions on the packet, and process for a few moments to knead the dough. Turn into a bowl, cover with oiled clear film and leave in a warm place for about half an hour, until doubled in size.

Divide the dough in half and roll out two rounds about 10 inches (25 cm) in diameter. Lift each on to a lightly greased baking tray. Spread the tomato sauce on to the bases. Process the marjoram until roughly chopped and sprinkle over the sauce.

Fit the grating disc and grate the two cheeses, then mix lightly together.

Fit the slicing disc and slice the green pepper and onion. Arrange the vegetables, pepperoni and olives on top of the pizzas. Sprinkle over the cheese. Cover with clear film and prove for 20 minutes, until the edges are puffy.

Heat the oven to 400°F/200°C/gas mark 6. Bake the pizzas for about 30 minutes, until the dough is golden.

Vegetables
and Salads

To get really good professional results when slicing vegetables in a processor it is necessary to pack the funnel neatly with long upright lengths of vegetables such as carrots, leeks, celery and cucumber. With cabbage, stand wedges close together in the feed tube and press down evenly with the plastic pusher. Peppers should be seeded, quartered and packed tightly together in the feeder.

When chopping onions using the metal blade, do not over-process. Watch them like a hawk, otherwise you can easily get onion purée rather than chopped onions!

Grating and slicing vegetables for salads is quick and efficient in the processor. Don't prepare them too far ahead, though, because they begin to lose nutrients as soon as they are cut. Also, salads containing cabbage or carrot may become too wet if left to stand.

Fresh Vegetables with Pesto

SERVES 4

Crisp seasonal vegetables with a rich sauce, good for a summer meal served with crusty bread. Pesto sauce gives the vegetables a delicious basil flavour and is available from supermarkets, usually in the past a section. Or make your own in the processor (see page 112).

VEGETABLE BASE
8 oz (225 g) onion
2 peppers, seeded
1 lb (450 g) courgettes
1 lb (450 g) tomatoes, skinned
1 tablespoon oil
knob of butter
2 cloves garlic, crushed
1 tablespoon Pesto (page 112)
salt
freshly ground black pepper

SAUCE TOPPING
1½ oz (40 g) butter
1½ oz (40 g) flour
¾ pint (450 ml) milk
1 teaspoon Dijon mustard
a little grated nutmeg
salt
freshly ground black pepper
1 egg, beaten
3 oz (75 g) Cheddar cheese

USING THE COARSE
SLICING DISC:
COARSE GRATING
DISC

Slice the vegetables and tomatoes in the processor, keeping each separate. Heat the oil and butter in a large non-stick frying pan and fry the onion and garlic until tender, then increase the heat and stir-fry all the vegetables except the tomatoes. Stir in the pesto sauce and seasoning. Turn into a large shallow ovenproof dish, top with sliced tomatoes and season well.

To make the sauce, melt the butter in a pan, add the flour and cook for about a minute. Blend in the milk and bring to the boil, stirring continuously until thickened, then season with mustard, nutmeg, salt and pepper. Remove the pan from the heat, stir in the egg and pour over the vegetables.

Heat the oven to 400°F/200°C/gas mark 6. Fit the grating disc and grate the cheese. Sprinkle over the sauce. Brown in the oven for about 20 minutes, then serve at once. Alternatively, brown under the grill.

Leeks and Potatoes Lavinia

SERVES 6

Layered sliced potatoes and leeks oven-baked until tender and crisp.

12 oz (350 g) leeks
salt
freshly ground black pepper
2 lb (900 g) potatoes, peeled
¾ pint (450 ml) good chicken stock

USING THE COARSE
SLICING DISC

Heat the oven to 400°F/200°C/gas mark 6 and grease a shallow oven-proof dish.

Slice the leeks in the processor and arrange half of them in the dish. Season lightly.

Cut potatoes lengthwise so that they fit into the funnel and slice, then arrange half of them on top of the leeks and season lightly. Add another layer of leeks and lastly top with potatoes. Pour over stock and cover with a lid or foil.

Bake in the top of the oven for 25 minutes, then remove the lid and cook for a further 25 minutes, until crisp, brown and tender.

Cabbage and Pepper Stir-Fry

SERVES 4–6

The preparation may be done well ahead but the stir-frying must be carried out just before serving so that the vegetables are still crisp. If you like them very *al dente*, shorten the cooking time.

1 spanish onion, cut into quarters
1 yellow pepper, seeded and cut into quarters
1 red pepper, seeded and cut into quarters
1 green pepper, seeded and cut into quarters
1 lb (450 g) white cabbage, cut into wedges
3 tablespoons olive oil
2 fat cloves garlic, crushed
salt
freshly ground black pepper

USING THE COARSE
SLICING DISC

Slice the onions in the processor. Stand the pepper quarters upright in the funnel two at a time and slice these too. Feed the cabbage wedges into the funnel and slice the cabbage.

Heat the oil in a large frying pan or wok, add the onion, garlic and peppers and stir-fry over a high heat for 3–4 minutes, tossing well with two wooden spatulas. Add the cabbage and continue cooking for a further couple of minutes over high heat, tossing well. Season with salt and pepper and serve at once.

Summer Courgettes

SERVES 4

An unusual way to serve courgettes. They have a lovely lemon flavour and are excellent with fish.

1 lb (450 g) courgettes
juice and grated rind of 1 lemon
2 oz (50 g) butter

USING THE COARSE
GRATING DISC

Cut a slice off each end of the courgettes and discard, then grate the courgettes in the processor. Put them in a bowl with the lemon juice and rind, toss well to distribute the lemon and leave as long as you can for the courgettes to absorb the flavour – preferably all day.

Heat the butter in a large frying pan or wok and add the courgettes together with any juice that is in the bowl. Fry quickly over maximum heat without colouring, until the courgettes are heated through and all the liquid has evaporated. This takes only a few minutes so the end result is dryish rather than a soggy mass. Serve immediately, piping hot.

Danish Red Cabbage

SERVES 6

A wonderful vegetable to go with ham, roast pork or grilled meat.

1 small red cabbage, cut into wedges
12 oz (350 g) cooking apples, peeled, cored and cut into quarters
5 tablespoons wine vinegar
1½ oz (40 g) demerara sugar
salt and freshly ground black pepper
1 oz (25 g) butter
1 tablespoon redcurrant jelly

USING THE COARSE
SLICING DISC

Slice the cabbage in the processor, then put it in a large saucepan. Slice apples and add them to the pan with the vinegar, sugar and seasoning. Cover and simmer for about 45 minutes, until the cabbage is tender.

When the cabbage is cooked add the butter and redcurrant jelly and stir until the butter has melted. Taste and check seasoning.

Glazed Carrots

SERVES 4

How to cheer up old carrots! If you wish to prepare a little ahead just keep the glazed carrots hot and add the parsley at the last moment.

1 lb (450 g) carrots
salt
1 oz (25 g) butter
freshly ground black pepper
1 level teaspoon caster sugar
small bunch of parsley

USING THE COARSE
SLICING DISC:
METAL BLADE

Slice the carrots in the processor. Transfer to a pan, cover with water and add a little salt. Bring to the boil, cover and simmer for 15–20 minutes, until just tender. Drain thoroughly.

Put the butter in the pan and add the drained carrots, seasoning and sugar. Toss over a high heat to glaze the carrots.

Fit the metal blade and chop the parsley in the processor. Turn the carrots into a warmed serving dish and sprinkle with chopped parsley to serve.

Puréed Vegetables

◆

A mixed dish of purées looks very attractive. There's a bonus too – they can be made ahead and reheated in the oven in a buttered dish covered with buttered foil. Vegetable purées also reheat successfully in a microwave. Cream can be added as well as butter, if liked.

USING THE METAL BLADE

Celeriac Purée

Cook equal quantities of celeriac and potato in boiling salted water until tender. Drain well, then turn into the processor bowl and process to a purée. Season to taste with salt and freshly ground black pepper and serve with a good knob of butter on top. Use carrots with potato as an alternative.

Sprout Purée

Cook the Brussels sprouts in boiling salted water until just tender. Drain well, then transfer to the processor bowl and process with 2 tablespoons of milk, salt and freshly ground black pepper. Heat a little butter in the bottom of a pan and reheat the purée in this before serving.

Swede Purée

Cook the swede in boiling salted water until tender. Drain well, then transfer to the processor bowl. Season well with salt and freshly ground black pepper, add a few knobs of butter and process until smooth. Serve with a knob of butter on top. Alternatively, use equal quantities of swede and carrot.

Parsnip Purée

Cook parsnips in boiling salted water until tender. Drain well then transfer to the processor bowl. Season with salt and freshly ground black pepper, add a few knobs of butter and process until smooth. Sprinkle with chopped parsley to serve.

Turnip Purée

Cook turnips in boiling salted water until tender. Drain well then transfer to the processor bowl. Season with salt and freshly ground black pepper, add a few knobs of butter and process until smooth. Sprinkle with chopped parsley to serve.

Potatoes Souflette

SERVES 6

Coarsely grated potato is enriched with butter and cream for special occasions. You can cook the potatoes a day ahead.

2 lb (900 g) even-sized potatoes
salt
freshly ground black pepper
1½ oz (40 g) butter, melted
¼ pint (150 ml) single cream

USING THE COARSE GRATING DISC

Boil the potatoes in their skins until barely tender and still firm in the centre. Drain and leave to get really cold.

Heat the oven to 425°F/220°C/gas mark 7 and butter a 2 pint (1 litre) shallow ovenproof dish really well.

Peel the potatoes, then grate them in the processor. Put a layer of potato into the dish, season and add more potato. Repeat until all the potato is used up. Do not press it down. Pour over the melted butter and cream.

Cook in the oven for about 30 minutes, until crisp and golden brown.

Dauphinois Potatoes

SERVES 4

A classic French recipe, simply made when using the processor.

1 lb (450 g) potatoes (Desirée or Edwards)
1 fat clove garlic
salt
freshly ground black pepper
¼ pint (150 ml) double cream
¼ pint (150 ml) milk
grated nutmeg
1½ oz (40 g) butter

USING THE FINE SLICING DISC

Heat the oven to 350°F/180°C/gas mark 4 and grease a shallow oven-proof dish.

Peel the potatoes and slice them thinly in the processor. Plunge the sliced potatoes in cold water to remove some of the starch, then dry them well in a clean towel or with kitchen paper.

Arrange a layer of half the potatoes in the dish, then add the crushed garlic, salt and pepper. Top with the remaining potatoes.

Mix together the cream and milk and pour over the potatoes. Sprinkle with grated nutmeg and dot the top with butter. Bake in the oven for about 1 hour, until the potatoes are tender and the top is nicely browned.

Rösti

♦

SERVES 4–6

A traditional Swiss snack or supper dish that can be served with a topping of fried eggs. It makes a good accompaniment to veal dishes, too.

2 lb (900 g) large potatoes
freshly ground black pepper
2 oz (50 g) butter

USING THE COARSE
GRATING DISC

Scrub the potatoes and boil in salted water for 10 minutes, until the outside is beginning to soften but the potato centre is still hard. Drain and cool, then peel and chill for several hours.

Grate the potatoes in the processor and season well. Melt half the butter in a non-stick frying pan and add the grated potato, flattening it down. Cook slowly over a low heat for about 20 minutes to brown the base.

Turn the potato cake upside down on to a plate. Melt the remaining butter in the pan and slide the potato cake back in to brown the second side. Slide on to a warm dish for serving.

Thatched Mashed Potatoes

SERVES 4

A delicious crispy topping mixed with herbs makes mashed potato really special. It's a good way to use up leftover jacket-baked potatoes.

>*2 lb (900 g) old potatoes, scrubbed and pricked*
>*about 3 tablespoons hot milk*
>*butter*
>*salt*
>*freshly ground black pepper*
>*bunch of fresh garden herbs such as chives, spring onions, basil*
>   *and marjoram*
>*2 oz (50 g) well-flavoured Cheddar cheese*

USING THE METAL
BLADE: COARSE
GRATING DISC

Heat the oven to 425°F/220°C/gas mark 7 and bake the potatoes for about 1½ hours, until soft in the middle. Cut the potatoes in half and allow to cool a little.

Scoop out the potato into a bowl, reserving the skins. Mash the potato with the milk, butter and seasoning and turn into a shallow ovenproof dish. Put the potato skins and herbs into the processor to chop up and mix together. Put to one side.

Fit the grating disc and grate the cheese in the processor. Mix the potato skins with the cheese and some salt and pepper and spoon on top of the mashed potato. Cook in the oven for about 20 minutes, until nicely brown on top and crispy.

Dhal

◆

SERVES 8

A traditional curry accompaniment. It freezes extremely well.

8 oz (225 g) red lentils
1 bay leaf
1 large carrot
1 large green pepper, seeded
1 large onion
2 tablespoons oil
½ inch (1.25 cm) piece fresh ginger root
½ level teaspoon ground cinnamon
½ level teaspoon ground cummin
½ level teaspoon ground coriander
14 oz (400 g) can peeled tomatoes
salt
freshly ground black pepper

USING THE METAL BLADE

Soak the lentils in cold water for 30 minutes, then drain and discard the water. Put the lentils in a saucepan and add sufficient cold water to cover. Bring to the boil, add the bay leaf and simmer for about 30 minutes, until the lentils are tender. Drain and discard the bay leaf.

Cut the vegetables into large chunks and put them in the processor bowl. Process until vegetables are finely chopped.

Heat the oil in a large pan, add the vegetables and fry for 5 minutes, stirring. Add the lentils, spices and tomatoes and cook gently until the carrots are soft.

Turn the mixture into the processor bowl and process briefly. It does not need to be completely smooth – some texture is nice.

Rinse out the saucepan, return mixture to the pan and reheat. Check seasoning and serve hot.

Cucumber and Dill Salad

◆

SERVES 10

A good accompaniment to fish and a refreshing salad for a summer buffet.

> 2 cucumbers
> bunch of fresh dill, washed and dried
> 2 tablespoons oil
> 4 tablespoons hot water
> 4 tablespoons white wine vinegar
> 4 tablespoons caster sugar
> salt
> freshly ground black pepper

USING THE COARSE
GRATING DISC:
METAL BLADE

Peel the cucumbers using a potato peeler, then slice them in the processor. If the cucumbers are too thick to go through the funnel, cut them in half lengthwise. Arrange in a serving dish.

Fit the metal blade and process the dill briefly. Remove from the processor bowl and set aside.

Put all the remaining ingredients in the processor bowl and process to mix. Check seasoning and pour over the cucumber. Sprinkle with dill and serve.

Coleslaw

◆

SERVES 8

Don't mix up the coleslaw too far ahead, otherwise the moisture from the vegetables will make the dressing too wet.

> 1 small white cabbage
> 1 small onion
> 2 carrots
> 4 tablespoons mayonnaise (page 67)
> 2 tablespoons French dressing (page 68)
> salt
> freshly ground black pepper
> 4 tablespoons Greek yoghurt
> 1 teaspoon Dijon mustard

USING THE COARSE
SLICING DISC: FINE
SLICING DISC:
COARSE GRATING
DISC

Remove the core from the cabbage. Cut the cabbage into pieces that will fit into the funnel and slice coarsely. Transfer to a large bowl. Fit the fine slicing disc, slice the onion and add to the bowl. Fit the coarse grating disc, grate the carrots and add them to the bowl, too.

Measure the mayonnaise, French dressing, seasoning, yoghurt and mustard into a bowl and mix together. Pour over the salad ingredients and mix well, then cover with clear film and refrigerate for an hour or so before serving.

Quick Salads

USING THE COARSE
GRATING DISC

Carrot Salad
Carrot is a quick salad to make when green salad ingredients are in short supply. Grate the carrots, toss in lemon juice and add a little ground coriander or cummin. Serve fairly quickly, otherwise a lot of juice will come out of the carrots.

USING THE COARSE
SLICING DISC

Red Cabbage Salad
Slice the red cabbage and toss in French dressing (page 68), perhaps with some added sultanas or currants. You can also mix it with some white cabbage, but don't leave to stand for too long because the colours will run.

USING THE COARSE
SLICING DISC

Crunchy Nut Salad
Slice some Brussels sprouts, white cabbage and half a leek in the processor. Add some chopped walnuts and toss in a mixture of equal quantities of mayonnaise (page 67) and plain yoghurt. Sprinkle with sunflower seeds before serving.

USING THE COARSE
SLICING DISC

Waldorf Salad
Slice thickly about 4 sticks celery in the processor. Quarter and core 2 red apples, then thickly slice in the processor. Mix together about 3 table-spoons homemade mayonnaise (page 67) and a tablespoon natural yoghurt. Mix the celery and apple with the yoghurt mayonnaise. Stir in 1 oz (25 g) chopped walnuts just before serving.

Sauces, Spreads and Stuffing

Many classic sauces can be made in a fraction of the time they normally take by using the processor. Bread sauce is no longer a chore as the processor makes short work of breadcrumbs, and mayonnaise (opposite) is dead easy!

Of course, none of us admits to making lumpy sauces. But if they do happen, a moment in the processor makes them smooth again.

Puréed fruit sauces are very good served cold with ice cream or hot with orange, lemon or vanilla soufflés. Raw strawberries, peaches and raspberries, sweetened with a little icing sugar, or blackcurrants, redcurrants, blackberries, gooseberries or apricots cooked in the minimum of water and sweetened to taste all make excellent puréed sauces. Raspberry, blackberry, currant and gooseberry purées need to be sieved but this is quick and easy when they have been processed first.

Mayonnaise

◆

MAKES ABOUT
1¾ PINTS (1 LITRE)

The method is foolproof and makes a very good mayonnaise. Made from whole eggs, it is a little less rich than one made using just yolks. If liked, replace half the sunflower oil with olive oil. For a thinner mayonnaise, add a little water or milk through the funnel with the motor running.

2 eggs, at room temperature
1 tablespoon wine vinegar
1 teaspoon caster sugar
1 teaspoon dry mustard
salt
freshly ground black pepper
1½ pints (900 ml) sunflower oil
juice of 1 large lemon

USING THE METAL
BLADE

Put all the ingredients except the oil and lemon juice into the processor bowl and process briefly to blend. With the machine running, add the oil through the funnel in a slow, steady stream until it has all been incorporated and the mixture is very thick. Switch on again and add all the lemon juice. Taste and check seasoning.

Turn out into jars and keep for up to a month in the refrigerator.

Variations

Aioli
This is the classic French garlic mayonnaise. Add two (or more, if you like) crushed cloves of garlic to the processor with the other ingredients.

Watercress Mayonnaise
Wash and roughly chop a bunch of watercress. Process briefly and stir into ½ pint (300 ml) of the made mayonnaise. Check seasoning.

Avocado Mayonnaise
Roughly chop the flesh of an avocado, put it in the processor bowl with a tablespoon of lemon juice and process briefly. Add ½ pint (300 ml) of the made mayonnaise and process very briefly to mix. Check seasoning.

Tartare Sauce
Put a rounded dessertspoon each of chopped gherkins and capers and a few sprigs of parsley in the processor bowl and process briefly. Add ½ pint (300 ml) of the made mayonnaise and process very briefly to mix.

Herb Mayonnaise
Wash and drain a generous handful of mixed fresh herbs. Process briefly. Add ½ pint (300 ml) of the made mayonnaise and process briefly to mix.

French Dressing

MAKES A GOOD
¾ PINT (450 ML)

Well worth making in the processor as it emulsifies and lasts better made this way. It is also quite marvellous when you are preparing vast quantities of salad for a party. Use olive oil instead of sunflower for special occasions, or a mixture of both.

> 1 clove garlic, crushed
> 1 teaspoon dry mustard
> salt
> freshly ground black pepper
> 2 tablespoons caster sugar
> ½ pint (300 ml) sunflower oil
> ¼ pint (150 ml) white or red wine vinegar

USING THE METAL
BLADE

Put all the ingredients into the processor bowl and process to combine. Processing for a longer time makes a thicker dressing, if that is how you like it.

Fresh Herb Cream Sauce

MAKES A GENEROUS
½ PINT (300 ML)

A wonderful fresh-tasting sauce ideal for serving with fish. It takes only seconds to combine the ingredients in the processor. Experiment with other fresh herbs to vary the flavour. You can also cook the sauce in the microwave on full power, stirring from time to time, until it has a coating consistency (about 3 minutes).

> 3 oz (75 g) butter, melted
> juice of 1 lemon
> 1 rounded teaspoon flour
> ½ pint (300 ml) single cream
> 1 egg yolk
> 1 tablespoon freshly snipped dill or chives
> salt
> freshly ground black pepper

USING THE METAL
BLADE

Measure all the ingredients except the herbs and seasoning into the processor bowl and process until smooth. Transfer to a small heatproof bowl. Set the bowl over a pan of simmering water and cook for about 10 minutes, stirring from time to time until the sauce has thickened and will coat the back of a spoon.

Stir in the herbs and season to taste. Pour into a serving bowl or sauceboat.

Hollandaise Sauce

♦

SERVES 4–6

Quick and easy made in the processor. If you have one of the new processors with a mini-bowl, it is wonderful for this. Instead of reduced vinegar, you can use lemon juice to flavour the sauce if you prefer. The best way of keeping Hollandaise warm is to transfer it to a small wide-necked vacuum flask until needed.

3 tablespoons white wine vinegar
1 tablespoon water
salt
freshly ground black pepper
5 egg yolks
8 oz (225 g) unsalted butter

USING THE METAL
BLADE

Combine the vinegar, water and seasoning in a small pan, bring to the boil and boil until about 1 tablespoon remains. Fill the processor bowl with boiling water to heat the bowl and blade, then throw the water away. Process the egg yolks until really smooth. Melt the butter until just boiling.

With the machine running, add the reduced vinegar and then the hot butter in a steady flow through the funnel. The sauce should look like thick mayonnaise. Should it not be as thick as you would like, heat gently in a heatproof bowl over a pan of simmering water, whisking until thicker.

Barbecue Sauce

SERVES 6

This sauce freezes well and is especially good with grilled chops, chicken joints or home-made beefburgers (page 38). It also cheers up bangers and mash.

1 medium-sized onion, cut into quarters
1 oz (25 g) butter
1 tablespoon oil
3 tablespoons water
2 tablespoons lemon juice
7 oz (200 g) can tomatoes
1 tablespoon brown sugar
2 teaspoons made mustard
½ teaspoon paprika
¼ teaspoon chilli powder
salt
freshly ground black pepper

USING THE METAL BLADE

Put the onion in the processor bowl and chop finely. Heat the butter and oil in a pan and gently fry the onion until soft. Add all the remaining ingredients, bring to the boil and simmer for about 20 minutes. Taste and check seasoning.

If you like a smooth sauce, return it to the processor and process before serving.

Tomato Coulis

MAKES ABOUT
½ PINT (300 ML)

A smooth purée sauce. Any left-over coulis can be frozen.

2 tablespoons olive oil
1 medium-sized onion, cut up roughly
1 lb (450 g) ripe tomatoes, cut into quarters
good sprig each of tarragon and thyme
1 fat clove garlic, crushed

USING THE METAL BLADE

Measure the oil, onion, tomatoes, herbs and garlic into a saucepan, and simmer slowly until pulpy. Remove the herbs, then transfer the sauce to the processor bowl and process until smooth. Rub through a sieve to remove the tomato skins and seeds. Taste and check seasoning.

Garlic Tomato Sauce

SERVES 4

This is a good sauce to serve with pasta and simple meat dishes or to use as a topping for pizzas. If using for a pizza, only process for a short time so that it is still chunky.

1 rasher streaky bacon, snipped
1 onion, cut into quarters
1 oz (25 g) flour
14 oz (400 g) can tomatoes
¼ pint (150 ml) stock
salt
freshly ground black pepper
1 tablespoon Worcestershire sauce
1 level teaspoon sugar
1 bay leaf
2 fat cloves garlic, crushed

USING THE METAL BLADE

Heat the bacon gently in a pan over a low heat until the fat begins to run out. Process the onion until roughly chopped, add to the bacon and cook gently for about 5 minutes.

Stir the flour into the onion and cook for a minute, then add the tomatoes and stock and bring to the boil, stirring until thickened. Stir in the remaining ingredients and cover with a lid. Simmer gently for about 30 minutes.

Remove the bay leaf, turn the sauce into the processor bowl and process to a purée. Rinse out the pan, then return the sauce to the pan and reheat. Taste and check seasoning before serving.

Fresh Tomato Sauce

MAKES ABOUT
2 PINTS (1.2 LITRES)

If you do not like the slightly rough consistency of the tomato pips, put the sauce through a coarse sieve before reheating.

2 lb (900 g) fresh tomatoes
1 large onion
2 small cloves garlic
2 oz (50 g) butter
1½ oz (40 g) flour
¾ pint (450 ml) chicken stock
2 bay leaves
2 cloves
1 tablespoon sugar
salt
freshly ground black pepper

USING THE METAL
BLADE

Put the tomatoes in a heatproof bowl and cover with boiling water. Leave for a few minutes, then drain and skin.

Put the onion and garlic in the processor bowl and process fairly finely. Melt the butter in a generous-sized pan, add the onion and garlic and soften for about 5 minutes. Stir in the flour and cook gently for a minute, then remove from heat.

Cut the tomatoes in half, or into quarters if they are large, and add to the pan. Stir well and blend in the stock. Add the bay leaves, cloves, sugar, salt and pepper and bring to the boil slowly, stirring until the sauce thickens. Cover and simmer for half an hour.

Remove from the heat and allow to cool a little. Process until smooth, then reheat and serve.

Quick Yoghurt Sauce

SERVES 6

Leafy herbs are the best to use for this light sauce. Serve with cold fish such as trout and salmon. For a richer sauce, use full-fat Greek yoghurt.

small bunch of fresh herbs, e.g. basil, tarragon, parsley and dill
juice of ½ lemon
½ pint (300 ml) natural yoghurt
salt
freshly ground black pepper

USING THE METAL
BLADE

Put the herbs in the processor and process for a few seconds until roughly chopped. Add the lemon juice, yoghurt and seasoning and process for a few seconds to mix.

Taste and check seasoning. Serve well chilled.

Vegetarian Gravy

◆

MAKES ABOUT
1 PINT (600 ML)

The soy sauce, which gives this gravy colour as well as flavour, is quite salty so you will probably not need to add extra seasoning. Do try to use a good-quality soy sauce – the best is shoyu, available from health-food shops. Serve with Vicarage Nut Roast (page 49) and other vegetarian dishes. If necessary, process the finished gravy for a moment or two to remove any lumps, then reheat gently.

> 1 onion, *cut into quarters*
> 2 *tablespoons oil*
> 2 *tablespoons flour*
> 1 *tablespoon tomato purée*
> 1 *pint (600 ml) good vegetable stock*
> *about 2 tablespoons soy sauce*

USING THE METAL
BLADE

Put the onion in the processor bowl and chop finely. Heat the oil in a saucepan, add the onion and cook until soft. Mix in the flour and cook for about 8 minutes, stirring from time to time, until lightly browned.

Stir the tomato purée into the flour and onions then gradually blend in the stock. Bring the gravy to the boil and simmer for 10 minutes. Remove the pan from the heat and stir in the soy sauce to taste. Reheat gently if necessary.

Garlic Butter

Use for making garlic bread, tossing through cooked vegetables, cooking mushrooms in or topping grilled steaks.

8 oz (225 g) butter
2 teaspoons fresh garlic purée (below), or 4 cloves garlic, crushed
salt
freshly ground black pepper

USING THE METAL
BLADE

Cut the butter into chunks and put it in the processor with the garlic purée and seasoning. Process for a few moments until smooth.
 Turn into a glass container, cover well and store in the refrigerator until required. It will keep for up to 1 month.

Variation

Garlic Herb Butter
Put a good bunch of fresh leafy herbs such as basil, marjoram, dill, tarragon and parsley into the processor and process for a few moments until roughly chopped. Then add the butter, garlic purée and seasoning and continue as above. Store in the refrigerator for up to 1 month.

Fresh Garlic Purée

Do use sparingly! It takes time to peel all the garlic but it is wonderful to have the purée ready to use without having to reach for a garlic crusher all the time. It also freezes well.

6 heads garlic
2 tablespoons oil

USING THE METAL
BLADE

Break the garlic heads down into cloves and peel. Put into the processor with the oil and process until to a smooth purée.
 Spoon into small glass jars, seal and store in the refrigerator for up to 6 weeks.

Rather a Good Stuffing

◆

MAKES ENOUGH TO
STUFF A 3½–4 LB
(1.6–1.8 kg) CHICKEN

Use for stuffing chicken or other meat. I use it to stuff the breast end of a chicken, loosening the skin over the end of the breast first.

> 2 oz (50 g) streaky bacon, snipped
> 1 large onion, cut into quarters
> 3 oz (75 g) shelled mixed nuts
> 2 oz (50 g) brown bread
> good bunch of parsley
> 1 egg
> salt
> freshly ground black pepper

USING THE METAL
BLADE

Heat the bacon gently in a non-stick pan until the fat begins to run out. Process the onion until roughly chopped, then add to the bacon and cook until the onion is softened and the bacon is cooked.

Put the nuts and bread into the processor bowl and process for a few moments. Add the parsley, onion mixture, egg and seasoning and process to bind.

Brandy Butter

◆

SERVES 8

Chilling the butter means that the mixture will absorb the brandy without curdling. If you can get concentrated butter, use it. You will find that you can add even more brandy! Serve with Christmas pudding and mince pies.

> 8 oz (225 g) butter, chilled
> 12 oz (350 g) icing sugar
> 6 tablespoons brandy

USING THE METAL
BLADE

Cut the butter into chunks. Put it in the processor bowl with the icing sugar and brandy and process for a few seconds until smoothly blended.

Turn the brandy butter into a serving dish and chill in the refrigerator to harden before serving. If made in advance, leave the butter at room temperature for about 30 minutes before serving.

Sandwich Fillings

<table>
<tr><td>USING THE METAL BLADE</td><td>The processor is wonderful for mixing bulk sandwich fillings. These are delicious with fresh granary bread and salad.</td></tr>
</table>

ENOUGH FOR 8
ROUNDS OF BREAD

Egg Mayonnaise

6 eggs, hard-boiled and shelled
2 tablespoons mayonnaise (page 67)
freshly ground black pepper

Put the eggs in the processor bowl and process for a few seconds until roughly chopped. Add the mayonnaise and seasoning and process just until mixed.

ENOUGH FOR 10
ROUNDS OF BREAD

Tuna and Celery

2 sticks celery, cut in 2 inch (5 cm) pieces
2 × 7 oz (200 g) cans tuna fish, drained
1 small green pepper, seeded and cut into quarters
3 tablespoons mayonnaise (page 67)
freshly ground black pepper

Put the celery and green pepper in the processor bowl and process until roughly chopped. Add the tuna, mayonnaise and black pepper and continue to process until just mixed.

ENOUGH FOR 8
ROUNDS OF BREAD

Cream Cheese and Herb

small bunch of fresh herbs such as chives, parsley, basil and
*   tarragon*
8 oz (225 g) cream cheese
freshly ground black pepper

Put the herbs in the processor bowl and process until roughly chopped. Add the cream cheese and pepper and continue to process until mixed.

Puddings

Sorbets and ice creams benefit from being made in the processor. They are frozen until just firm, then processed to break up any ice crystals and returned to the freezer. I find it easier to do this in two or three batches. The results are smooth and easy to scoop. Ices with a high proportion of water will finally need to be thawed for a short time in the refrigerator before serving.

Breadcrumb-based puddings could hardly be simpler when you have a processor. One of the smartest is Chocolate Mocha Indulgence (page 82), with its layers of chocolatey crumbs and whipped cream. And Lemon Passion Flan (page 89) on a crunchy biscuit base sounds too easy to be true – it's well worth trying!

The quickest puddings of all to make in the processor must be fruit fools – see page 91 for some almost instant suggestions.

French Apple Flan

◆

SERVES 6–8

The addition of an egg yolk and sugar makes a rich crisp pastry for this classic French tart. It is a very soft pastry to handle if it's not chilled before rolling. Add ½ teaspoon vanilla essence to the confectioner's custard if you haven't any vanilla sugar.

PASTRY
6 oz (175 g) plain flour
½ oz (15 g) caster sugar
4 oz (100 g) butter, cut in pieces
1 egg yolk
2 teaspoons cold water

CONFECTIONER'S CUSTARD
4 oz (100 g) vanilla sugar
3 level tablespoons cornflour
¾ pint (450 ml) milk
4 egg yolks

TOPPING
1½ lb (675 g) cooking apples, peeled and cored
2 oz (50 g) butter
2 oz (50 g) demerara sugar

USING THE METAL
BLADE: COARSE
SLICING DISC

First make the pastry. Measure the flour, sugar and butter into the processor bowl and process until the mixture resembles fine breadcrumbs. Mix together the egg yolk and water. With the machine running, add to the bowl through the funnel. Process just until a ball of dough forms, which will take only seconds.

Roll out the pastry on a floured surface and use to line a 9 inch (23 cm) flan tin. Chill for 30 minutes.

Put a thick baking sheet in the oven and heat the oven to 425°F/220°C/ gas mark 7. Line the flan with greaseproof paper, weight down with baking beans and bake blind for 15 minutes. Remove the paper and beans after 10 minutes and return the flan to the oven to dry out.

Meanwhile, prepare the confectioner's custard for the filling. Put the vanilla sugar and cornflour in a saucepan and blend with a little of the milk. Add the remaining milk and bring to the boil, stirring all the time, until the mixture thickens. Cook for a minute.

Remove the pan from the heat and beat in the egg yolks one at a time. Return the pan to the heat and cook very gently for 5 minutes, stirring continuously. Do not allow to boil. Remove from the heat and leave to cool, then pour into the pastry shell.

Fit the slicing disc and slice the apples. Melt the butter in a large frying pan. Add the apple slices, sprinkle with sugar and cook over a moderate heat, tossing gently, until they are almost tender. Arrange them in an overlapping pattern on top of the flan. Some pieces may be a little too chunky, so pick out the best slices for the top. Serve warm or cold.

Plum and Almond Crumble

SERVES 4

Vary the fruit as the seasons come round. Apples, gooseberries and rhubarb all make good crumbles – omit the flaked almonds if using these fruits. This is equally good served with custard or cream.

1½ lb (675 g) plums, washed, halved and stoned
4 oz (100 g) sugar
1 oz (25 g) flaked almonds
1 quantity Crumble Topping (page 96)

USING THE METAL BLADE

Heat the oven to 400°F/200°C/gas mark 6. Put the plums in the bottom of a 2 pint (1.2 litre) oval ovenproof dish and sprinkle with the sugar and flaked almonds. Cover the fruit generously with crumble topping.

Bake in the oven for about 40 minutes, until the crumble is nicely brown and the fruit is tender.

Variation

Plum and Apple Crumble

Replace some of the plums with apple, and add a little cinnamon and brown sugar or the juice and finely grated rind of a lemon. To give more texture to the crumble add a couple of tablespoons of porridge oats.

Cinnamon Apple Pancakes

SERVES 4

These pancakes can be made and filled in advance, then crisped in the oven before serving. Sprinkle with cinnamon and sugar and serve hot with whipped cream or ice cream.

APPLE FILLING
4 large Bramley apples, peeled, cored and cut into quarters
¼ teaspoon ground cinnamon
6 oz (175 g) demerara sugar
good knob of butter

BATTER
4 oz (100 g) flour
1 egg
½ pint (300 ml) milk and water, mixed
1 tablespoon sunflower oil plus oil for frying

a little melted butter
sugar
cinnamon

USING THE COARSE
SLICING DISC:
METAL BLADE

Slice the apples in the processor. Measure all the ingredients for the apple filling into a saucepan, mix well and cook slowly until the apples are tender, stirring occasionally. Allow to cool.

Fit the metal blade. Put all the batter ingredients in the processor bowl and process until smooth. Scrape down the sides of the bowl and briefly reprocess. Pour the batter into a jug.

Heat a little oil in an 8 inch (20 cm) frying pan. When the oil is hot, pour off any excess and add about 2 tablespoons of batter to the pan. Tip and rotate the pan so that the batter spreads out evenly and covers the base. Cook for about a minute, until pale brown underneath, then turn over with a palette knife and cook for about another minute. Slip the pancake out of the pan and set to one side. Make about seven more pancakes with the remaining batter.

Heat the oven to 400°F/200°C/gas mark 6. Divide the apple filling among the pancakes and roll them up, folding in the ends to form a neat parcel. Transfer the rolled pancakes to a roasting tin, brush them with melted butter and heat through in the oven for about 20 minutes, until hot and crisp. Arrange on a serving dish and dust with sugar and cinnamon.

FACING PAGE: *Filo Cases with Chicken and Vegetable Stir-Fry (page 46)*

Coffee Cream Pancakes

◆

SERVES 6–8

These thin pancakes are ideally made in a non-stick pan or in a very lightly greased ordinary frying pan. They are served cold, filled with whipped cream and jam. Extra pancakes can be wrapped in foil and frozen before the filling is added.

> 4 oz (100 g) self-raising flour
> ½ oz (15 g) sugar
> 2 eggs
> ½ pint (300 ml) milk and water, mixed
> 1 tablespoon strong black coffee
> 3 teaspoons vanilla essence
> 2 oz (50 g) butter, melted
> ½ pint (300 ml) whipping cream
> jam
> icing sugar, for dusting

USING THE METAL BLADE

Measure the flour and sugar into the processor bowl. In a jug, mix together the eggs, milk and water, coffee, vanilla essence and melted butter. With the machine running, add the contents of the jug through the funnel and process until the batter is smooth. If the batter is too thick, add a little more water to thin it down. Pour the batter back into the jug.

Heat a non-stick frying pan. Spoon about a tablespoon of batter into the pan and tip and rotate it so that the batter spreads out and evenly coats the base. Cook for about a minute, then turn the pancake over with a palette knife and cook the other side briefly. Slip the pancake out of the pan and put to one side to cool. Make about 18 more pancakes with the remaining batter.

When all the batter is used up, spread the middle of each pancake with some whipped cream and a little jam. Fold them up or pinch them to look like little brown bags. Serve cold, dusted lightly with icing sugar.

FACING PAGE, CLOCKWISE FROM TOP: *Blackberry Mousse (page 83), Coffee Cream Pancakes (above), American Cheesecake (page 88)*

Dorset Apple Cake

SERVES 6–8

A very moist cake that is delicious served hot or cold.

10 oz (275 g) self-raising flour
8 oz (225 g) demerara sugar
4 oz (100 g) soft margarine
2 eggs
6 fl oz (175 ml) milk
1 level teaspoon ground cinnamon
8 oz (225 g) cooking apples, peeled and cut up roughly
2 oz (50 g) sultanas
extra sugar, for dredging

USING THE METAL
BLADE

Heat the oven to 350°F/180°C/gas mark 4 and grease and line an 8 inch (20 cm) round cake tin. Measure the flour, sugar, margarine, eggs, milk and cinnamon into the processor bowl and process for 30–40 seconds. Scrape down the sides of the bowl and process for a further 10 seconds. Add the apples and sultanas and process for about 5 seconds, just to mix them in but not to chop them.

   Pour the mixture into the prepared tin. Sprinkle with demerara sugar and bake for 1–1½ hours, until the cake is golden and risen. Serve warm with whipped cream.

Chocolate Mocha Indulgence

SERVES 6

Best made in small wine glasses so the different layers can be seen.

4 oz (100 g) fresh brown bread
3 oz (75 g) demerara sugar
4 generous tablespoons drinking chocolate
1 level tablespoon instant coffee
½ pint (300 ml) double cream
¼ pint (150 ml) single cream

USING THE METAL
BLADE

Break the bread into pieces and process in the machine to form quite fine crumbs. Add the sugar, drinking chocolate and coffee to the processor bowl and process very briefly, just enough to mix thoroughly.

Measure the two creams into a bowl and whisk together until they form soft peaks. Divide half the chocolate mixture among six wine glasses, cover with a generous half of the cream, then add the remaining chocolate mixture. Top with the remaining cream and chill in the refrigerator for at least 6 hours.

Blackberry Mousse

SERVES 8

Take care not to cook the blackberries for too long, otherwise they will lose their bright colour.

> ³/₄ oz (20 g) powdered gelatine
> 4 tablespoons cold water
> 1¹/₂ lb (675 g) blackberries
> juice of 1 lemon
> 4 eggs, separated
> 4 oz (100 g) sugar
> ¹/₂ pint (300 ml) whipping cream, whipped

USING THE METAL
BLADE

Put the gelatine and water in a small bowl and leave to become spongy. Stand the bowl in a pan of simmering water and leave to become clear.

Meanwhile measure the blackberries into a pan, keeping back eight for decoration. Add the lemon juice and cook over a low heat until the juices come out, then increase the heat a little and cook until the fruit is soft.

Purée the blackberries in the processor, then sieve the purée to remove the seeds. Stir the dissolved gelatine into the hot purée.

Rinse out the processor bowl. Put the egg yolks and sugar in the processor bowl and process for a few moments, then add the hot purée and mix well. Allow to cool and fold in the whisked egg whites and two thirds of the cream. Pour into a 2 pint (1.2 litre) glass dish or individual glasses and leave to set in the refrigerator.

Decorate with the remaining cream and blackberries just before serving.

Variation

Blackcurrant Mousse
The mousse can also be made using blackcurrants. Remove the stems before cooking the fruit and proceed as above.

Fresh Orange and Peach Mousse

SERVES 6

A sharp tasting mousse that is well worth making for a party. If it will have to be out of the refrigerator for some time before serving, use twice as much gelatine.

4 oz (100 g) dried peaches
¼ pint (300 ml) water
½ oz (12.5 g) powdered gelatine
½ pint (300 ml) fresh orange juice
2 eggs separated, the whites whisked
2 oz (50 g) caster sugar
6 fl oz (175 ml) whipping cream, whipped

USING THE METAL BLADE

Put the peaches in a bowl with the water and leave to soak overnight. Transfer to a saucepan and simmer gently for 10 minutes, or until tender. Saving the liquid in a jug, drain the peaches and purée them in the processor. Add the liquid through the funnel with the machine running, then set aside to cool.

Put the gelatine and 2 tablespoons of the fresh orange juice in a small bowl. Allow to stand for about 3 minutes to form a sponge, then stand the bowl in a pan of simmering water until the gelatine has completely dissolved.

Warm the processor bowl and the metal blade slightly by pouring boiling water over them. Discard the water then process the yolks and caster sugar until they begin to thicken slightly. Add the cooled gelatine, peach purée, remaining orange juice, half of the whipped cream and the whisked egg whites. Process very briefly to mix well, then pour into a large glass serving bowl. Leave to set in the fridge then decorate with the rest of the whipped cream.

Rhubarb Sorbet

SERVES 6

A refreshing and simple way to use up homegrown rhubarb. Serve with brandy snaps.

½ pint (300 ml) water
6 oz (175 g) caster sugar
2 lb (900 g) rhubarb, washed
sugar
grated rind and juice of 1 orange
juice of 1 lemon

USING THE COARSE
SLICING DISC:
METAL BLADE

Measure the water and caster sugar into a saucepan and bring to the boil. Boil over high heat for 5 minutes, then leave to cool.

Slice the rhubarb in the processor. Combine the rhubarb, 1 tablespoon of the syrup, about 1 tablespoon of sugar and the orange rind in a saucepan and cook until the rhubarb is tender. Taste and add more sugar if necessary. Stir in the lemon and orange juice.

Fit the metal blade and purée the rhubarb mixture with the remaining syrup. Pour into shallow containers and freeze until large ice crystals have formed but the sorbet is not altogether solid.

Break up the half-frozen mixture and turn it into the processor bowl. Process until just smooth, then return to the containers and freeze until solid. Repeat the process.

Using an ice-cream scoop, serve in pretty glasses.

Gooseberry Sorbet

SERVES 6

No need to top and tail the gooseberries because after processing they are quick to sieve. If you have any elderflower blossoms you can add two or three to the gooseberries when cooking, for a delicate flavour. Serve with shortbread biscuits.

½ pint (300 ml) water
6 oz (175 g) caster sugar
1½ lb (675 g) gooseberries
sugar
juice of 1½ lemons

USING THE METAL
BLADE

Measure the water and caster sugar into a saucepan and bring to the boil. Keep at a steady boil for 5 minutes, then leave to cool.

Put the gooseberries in a saucepan with about a tablespoon of sugar and a tablespoon of the syrup. Cook until soft. Process the gooseberries until smooth, then sieve the purée.

Combine the sieved purée with the rest of the sugar syrup and add the lemon juice. Taste and add more sugar if necessary. Pour into a shallow container and freeze until ice crystals form but the sorbet is not altogether solid.

Break up the half-frozen mixture and turn it into the processor bowl. Process until just smooth, then return to the container and freeze until solid. Repeat the process.

Serve the sorbet in pretty glasses.

Brown Bread Ice Cream

SERVES 8

A wonderful ice cream with crunchy pieces of crisp caramelised bread-crumbs running through it. Take care not to get the silicone paper too near to the grill when toasting the crumbs, otherwise it could catch light. The beauty of this ice cream is that there's no need to process it once frozen.

CARAMEL
2 oz (50 g) brown bread
4 oz (100 g) demerara sugar

ICE CREAM
4 eggs
4 oz (100 g) caster sugar
½ pint (300 ml) whipping cream, lightly whipped

USING THE METAL BLADE

Cover a large baking sheet with a sheet of non-stick silicone paper. Put the bread for the caramel into the processor and process to form fine breadcrumbs. Scatter the breadcrumbs over the silicone paper then sprinkle with the demerara sugar. Heat under a medium grill, letting the sugar melt and turning the breadcrumbs every few minutes, until a deep straw colour. Leave to become cold, then turn into the processor and process for a few moments, until crushed.

To make the ice cream, separate the eggs, putting the whites in a large bowl and the yolks in a small bowl. Whisk the whites with an electric whisk until stiff, then add the sugar a teaspoon at a time, whisking on full speed. Blend the yolks with a fork and fold into the meringue. Lastly, fold in the cream and crushed caramelised breadcrumbs.

Turn into a 2½ pint (1.5 litre) shallow plastic container. Cover and freeze.

Allow the ice cream to stand at room temperature for about 5 minutes before scooping out and serving.

Apricot Flummery

SERVES 12

A very refreshing and light dessert. Serve with small brandy snaps or Lemon Finger Biscuits (page 104).

8 oz (225 g) dried apricots
1 pint (600 ml) warm water
juice of 1 lemon
12 oz (350 g) caster sugar
1 pint (600 ml) milk
½ pint (300 ml) double cream, lightly whipped
sprigs of mint or borage and blobs of whipped cream, to decorate

USING THE METAL BLADE

Put the apricots in a bowl with the warm water and leave to soak overnight. Transfer to a saucepan, bring to the boil and simmer, covered, until tender. Cool, then drain off the liquid.

Process the apricots with the lemon juice until smooth. Blend together the whipped cream, apricot purée, sugar and milk and mix well. Turn into a flat-bottomed plastic container, cover and freeze until almost solid.

Spoon out pieces into the processor and process until smooth. Pour into 12 ramekins or one 2 pint (1.2 litre) straight-sided dish that will go in the freezer and freeze.

Thaw individual dishes for 5 minutes or a larger dish for 15 minutes before serving. Decorate with fresh mint and blobs of cream.

American Cheesecake

SERVES 6–8

A no-cook cheesecake that's easy to make and heaven to eat. Do not freeze the cheesecake mixture as it would crack and separate on thawing.

FLAN CASE
6 oz (175 g) digestive biscuits
3 oz (75 g) butter
1½ oz (40 g) demerara sugar

FILLING
12 oz (350 g) cream cheese
1 oz (25 g) caster sugar
¼ pint (150 ml) double cream
¼ pint (150 ml) Greek yoghurt
juice of 1½ lemons

TOPPING
6 oz (175 g) soft fruit
4 tablespoons redcurrant jelly

USING THE METAL BLADE

Process the biscuits briefly, being very careful not to reduce them to a paste. Melt the butter in a saucepan, stir in the demerara sugar, then remove from the heat and stir in the crushed biscuits and press over the base of an 8 inch (20 cm) loose-bottomed cake tin using a metal spoon. Set aside.

For the filling, measure the cream cheese and sugar into the processor bowl and process just enough to combine, then add the double cream and yoghurt and process briefly again. With the machine running, pour in the lemon juice through the funnel. Turn the mixture into the cake tin and put in the refrigerator to chill and set.

Arrange the fruit on the top of the cheesecake (if using strawberries, cut them in half). Heat the redcurrant jelly in a small saucepan until it has melted and brush it carefully over the fruit. Leave to set.

Lemon Passion Flan

SERVES 6

Really easy to make and loved by all ages. It can be covered with a layer of soft fresh fruit such as strawberries, raspberries or red currants. Do not overprocess the crumbs so that they are like flour.

BISCUIT BASE
4 ginger biscuits
4 digestive biscuits
2 oz (50 g) butter
1 level tablespoon demerara sugar

FILLING
14 oz (400 g) can condensed milk
¼ pint (150 ml) double cream
juice of 2 lemons
fruit to decorate

USING THE METAL
BLADE

Process the ginger biscuits then add the digestive biscuits and process for a few seconds more.

Melt the butter in a saucepan and add the sugar, then remove from the heat and stir in the crushed biscuits. Mix well and press over the base and sides of a 7 inch (17.5 cm) flan ring or loose-bottomed flan tin. Spread evenly and press down with the back of a metal spoon.

To make the filling, put the condensed milk, cream and lemon juice in a bowl and whisk together until well blended. Pour into the flan case and chill in the refrigerator for several hours.

To serve, remove the flan ring and decorate the top with fruit.

Chocolate Profiteroles

MAKES 20
PROFITEROLES

A blissful dessert! Don't fill and ice more than 6 hours ahead, otherwise the result will be soggy.

1 quantity Choux Pastry dough (page 95)
½ pint (300 ml) whipping cream

CHOCOLATE ICING
2 oz (50 g) butter
2 oz (50 g) cocoa, sifted
8 oz (225 g) icing sugar
about 2 tablespoons milk

USING THE METAL
BLADE

Heat the oven to 400°F/200°C/gas mark 6 and grease 2 baking sheets.

Put the pastry dough into a piping bag fitted with ½ inch (1.25 cm) plain nozzle and pipe about 20 profiteroles on to the baking sheets. Bake in oven for about 20 minutes, until well risen and golden. Remove from the oven and turn the heat down to 350°F/180°C/gas mark 4. Make a small hole in each with a pointed knife to let the steam out, then return them to the oven for about 10 minutes to dry out. Leave to cool.

Split each profiterole and fill with whipped cream. For the icing, measure the butter into a pan, heat gently until melted then add the cocoa and cook for a minute. Transfer the chocolate mixture to the processor. Add the icing sugar and a little of the milk and process until smooth, adding a little more milk if necessary. Dip each profiterole in icing and leave to set.

Variation

Coffee-Iced Profiteroles

1 oz (25 g) butter
very strong coffee
8 oz (225 g) icing sugar, sieved
cream-filled profiteroles, as above

USING THE METAL
BLADE

Measure the butter and 1 tablespoon of coffee into a small pan and allow the butter to melt over a low heat. Transfer to the processor bowl, add the icing sugar and process until smooth, adding a little more coffee to give a coating consistency. Dip each profiterole in icing and leave to set.

Quick Processor Puddings

ALL SERVE 4

Cheating, but very quick!

USING THE METAL
BLADE

Peach Fool
Drain a can of peaches. Put the fruit in the processor bowl with a can of custard and the juice of an orange and process until smooth. Pour into individual glasses and serve chilled.

Coffee Cream
Put a can of custard in the processor bowl with 3 teaspoons instant coffee and process until blended. Add ½ pint (300 ml) double cream, 1 tablespoon caster sugar and 2 tablespoons brandy. Turn into individual glasses and serve chilled.

Creamy Raspberry Fool
Measure ½ pint (300 ml) fresh raspberry purée into the processor bowl. Cut a small block of vanilla ice cream into chunks, add to the processor bowl and process together until smooth. Pour into individual glasses and serve straight away.

Pastry
and Crumbles

◆

You will have success every time if you make your pastry in the processor. In fact it's foolproof. The fat and flour are rubbed in in the processor bowl using the metal blade, then just enough liquid is added through the funnel to bind the pastry to a ball round the blade. It helps if the fat is chilled first.

You will find that pastry made in the processor requires slightly less liquid than pastry made by hand, and pastry made with a proportion of wholemeal flour will absorb more liquid than pastry made with white flour.

A word of warning: do not process any pastry for longer than necessary. Process just until it forms a ball round the blade, then stop. Lengthy overprocessing gives a tough result that will shrink when cooked.

Shortcrust Pastry

◆

The processor produces a trouble-free crisp short pastry because it is not overhandled. Amounts given here will make a top and base for an 8 inch (20 cm) pie or two 8 inch (20 cm) flan cases.

> *8 oz (225 g) flour*
> *4 oz (100 g) hard margarine or butter, cut into pieces*
> *2 tablespoons water*

USING THE METAL BLADE

Measure the flour into the processor bowl. Add the margarine and process until the mixture resembles fine breadcrumbs. With the machine running add the water through the funnel and process until the dough forms a ball.

Wrap and rest the pastry in the refrigerator and use in the normal way.

Fast Flaky Pastry

◆

An excellent pastry for steak and kidney, fish and fruit pies. It can also be used for Eccles cakes and sausage rolls. The processor is used for grating the block margarine quickly and easily before it has time to soften; the pastry itself requires very little processing. The ingredients given will be enough to make the top of a large pie and some decoration.

> *6 oz (175 g) hard margarine, straight from the freezer*
> *8 oz (225 g) strong plain flour*
> *scant ¼ pint (150 ml) cold water*

USING THE COARSE GRATING DISC: METAL BLADE

Grate the frozen margarine in the processor and put it in the fridge to keep very cold.

Fit the metal blade. Measure the flour into the processor bowl, add the margarine and a little water and process very briefly, adding more water through the funnel until the mixture forms a dough. Switch off immediately; be careful not to overprocess or the pastry will not be flaky.

Roll on a lightly floured board to make a strip ½ inch (1.25 cm) thick and 6 inches (15 cm) wide. Fold pastry in three and give it a quarter turn to the left. Repeat the rolling and folding process once more. Chill before using.

Hot-Water Crust Pastry

This pastry is lovely for cold savoury pies to take on summer picnics or serve at Christmas feasts. It is easy to make and beautifully crisp. It makes enough for a raised pie in a 2 lb (900 g) loaf tin.

12 oz (350 g) plain flour
5 oz (150 g) white vegetable fat
¼ pint (150 ml) plus 2 tablespoons water

USING THE METAL
BLADE

Put the flour in the processor bowl. In a saucepan, melt the lard with the water and when melted pour into the processor through the funnel with the motor switched on. Process until a smooth dough forms.

Allow the pastry to become cool enough to handle before using.

Pâte Brisée

This is the French version of shortcrust pastry, and it is crisper and richer than ours. Use for savoury dishes and quiches. If made with butter it will have a lovely flavour. These quantities will make enough to line a 9 inch (22.5cm) flan tin or two 6 inch (15 cm) flan tins.

6 oz (175 g) plain flour
4 oz (100 g) butter, cut into pieces
1 tablespoon cold water
1 egg yolk

USING THE METAL
BLADE

Measure the flour into the processor bowl, add the butter and process until the mixture resembles fine breadcrumbs. Blend the water with the egg yolk. Pour in through the funnel with the machine running and process until the dough forms a ball. Scrape down the sides of the bowl if necessary.

Roll out the dough on a lightly floured surface and use to line a flan tin. Chill in the refrigerator for 15 minutes. Put a baking sheet in the oven and heat the oven to 425°F/220°C/gas mark 7.

Line the flan with greaseproof paper, weight down with baking beans and bake blind on the baking sheet for 20–25 minutes, until the pastry is golden brown at the edges and crisp. Remove the paper and beans for the last 10 minutes of baking to dry out the base of the case.

Variation

Sweet Pâte Brisée

For a sweet version of this pastry, add 1 tablespoon caster sugar to the flour and butter before processing.

Choux Pastry

This is an easy pastry to make in the processor as the machine does all the beating for you. It also enables you to produce larger quantities than would be feasible by hand, but choux dough won't keep so you will need to use it all in one go. It is used for sweet or savoury eclairs and profiteroles (see page 90). Remember to space the pastry shapes well apart on the baking sheets, as choux pastry items increase in volume.

> *2 oz (50 g) butter*
> *¼ pint (150 ml) water*
> *2½ oz (65 g) plain flour*
> *2 eggs, beaten*

USING THE METAL
BLADE

Heat the oven to 400°F/200°C/gas mark 6 and grease two baking sheets.

Put the butter and water into a small pan and bring slowly to the boil, to allow the butter to melt. Measure the flour into the processor bowl, switch the processor on and with machine running pour the liquid in through the funnel. Process until a smooth dough forms. Scrape down the sides of the bowl, then switch on again, add the beaten eggs through the funnel and process until the mixture is smooth and shiny. The pastry is then ready to use and can either be piped or dropped in small amounts from two teaspoons on to the prepared baking sheets.

Bake in the oven for about 20 minutes, until golden brown and risen. Remove from oven and reduce the heat to 350°F/180°C/gas mark 4. Make a slit in each one to allow the steam to escape, then return to the oven for about 10 minutes to dry out. Cool on a wire tray.

Crumble Topping

A versatile mixture which can be used to top lots of sweet fruit puddings, or, with the sugar omitted, makes a nice change for a fish pie. Demerara gives a crunchier texture than granulated sugar. It is so easy to make a large amount very quickly in the processor and store it in the freezer. Just multiply the amounts given for making large freezer quantities. Store in the refrigerator for up to 1 month or freeze for up to 3 months. There's no need to thaw it before use.

6 oz (175 g) flour
3 oz (75 g) margarine
2 oz (50 g) demerara or granulated sugar

USING THE METAL BLADE

Measure all the ingredients into the processor bowl and process until the mixture resembles coarse breadcrumbs.

Variation

Oatmeal Crumble
Replace 3 oz (75 g) of the flour with the same weight of rolled oats.

Almond Crumble
Add 1 oz (25 g) flaked almonds to the mixture after processing.

Savoury Crumble
Omit the sugar and add 2 oz (50 g) grated well-flavoured Cheddar cheese to the mixture before processing. Use to top minced meat pies or fish pies instead of pastry.

FACING PAGE, CLOCKWISE FROM BACK: *Elderflower Champagne (page 125)*, *Spicy Samosas (page 122)*, *Flaky Cheese Crisps (page 118)*, *Spiced Mango and Cheese Dip (page 115)*

OPPOSITE PAGE 97, TOP TO BOTTOM: *Lemon Crunchy Loaf (page 101)*, *Family Fruit Traybake (page 98)*, *Butter Shortbread (page 102)*

Cakes
and Bread

Cake-making is highly successful in the processor. The best method is the all-in-one method, where the ingredients are measured into the processor bowl and mixed together in one go.

If fruit is added to a cake mixture, add it at the end and process for only a moment, just long enough to mix. If processed for longer you could end up with a grey mixture and finely chopped fruit!

For larger amounts of cake mixture – using more than six eggs – process in batches so as not to strain the machine.

When making icing for family cakes, you can get a marvellously smooth result with so little effort in the processor. You don't even need to sieve the icing sugar first.

The processor takes all the hard work out of bread-making too. It kneads perfectly in a fraction of the time it takes to do it by hand.

Victoria Sandwich

Probably the best-known English cake.

6 oz (150 g) soft margarine
6 oz (150 g) caster sugar
3 eggs
6 oz (150 g) self-raising flour
1 level teaspoon baking powder
3 tablespoons raspberry jam
caster sugar, for decoration

USING THE METAL
BLADE

Heat the oven to 350°F/180°C/gas mark 4. Grease and line the base of two 7 inch (17 cm) straight-sided sandwich tins with greased greaseproof paper.

Measure the margarine, sugar, eggs, flour and baking powder into the processor bowl and process for a few seconds to mix. Scrape down the sides of the bowl and reprocess briefly. Divide the mixture between the prepared tins, spread level and bake for 25–30 minutes, until pale golden and springy to touch.

Cool slightly, then turn out on to a wire rack to cool completely.

Spread one cake with jam, top with the other cake and sprinkle with caster sugar.

Variations

Chocolate
Blend 3 tablespoons cocoa with 4 tablespoons hot water and add to the bowl with all the other ingredients before processing.

Lemon
Add the finely grated rind of a lemon to the other ingredients before processing.

Family Fruit Traybake

MAKES 21 PIECES

Quick and easy to make. Take great care only to process the fruit for a moment, just to mix, otherwise it will be chopped.

6 oz (175 g) soft margarine
8 oz (225 g) self-raising flour
1½ level teaspoons baking powder
6 oz (175 g) caster sugar
3 eggs
2 tablespoons milk
8 oz (225 g) mixed fruit
2 level tablespoons demerara sugar

USING THE METAL BLADE

Heat the oven to 350°F/180°C/gas mark 4. Grease and line a 12 × 9 inch (30 × 23 cm) roasting tin with greased greaseproof paper.

Measure the margarine, flour, baking powder, caster sugar, eggs and milk into the processor bowl and process for a few seconds to mix. Scrape down the sides of the bowl, add the fruit and process for just a moment to mix. Turn into the tin and level the top.

Bake in the oven for about 20 minutes. Sprinkle the demerara sugar evenly over the top of the cake and return to the oven for a further 15–20 minutes, until the cake has shrunk slightly from the sides of the tin and is well risen. Leave to cool in the tin. Cut into pieces to serve.

Mincemeat Traybake

MAKES 21 PIECES

Very moist and fruity with a crunchy topping.

5 oz (150 g) soft margarine
5 oz (150 g) light soft brown sugar
2 eggs
8 oz (225 g) self-raising flour
4 oz (100 g) currants
1 lb (450 g) mincemeat
3 oz (75 g) demerara sugar

USING THE METAL BLADE

Heat the oven to 350°F/180°C/gas mark 4. Grease and line a 12 × 9 inch (30 × 23 cm) roasting tin with greased greaseproof paper.

Measure the margarine, soft brown sugar, eggs and flour into the processor bowl and process for a few moments to mix. Scrape down the sides of the bowl, add the mincemeat and currants and process for a few more moments until just mixed in.

Turn into the prepared tin and bake for 20 minutes. Sprinkle over the demerara sugar and bake for a further 15 minutes, until golden brown and shrinking away from the sides of the tin. Leave to cool in the tin.

Chocolate Traybake

MAKES 21 PIECES

The icing on this traybake stays glossy when dry and looks so inviting! If you line the tin with foil you can lift it out, complete with cake, ready for icing, and leave your tin free for another use.

6½ oz (185 g) self-raising flour
2 level tablespoons cocoa
1 level teaspoon baking powder
5 oz (150 g) caster sugar
2 level tablespoons golden syrup
2 large eggs
¼ pint (150 ml) sunflower oil
¼ pint (150 ml) milk

CHOCOLATE ICING
4 oz (100 g) Bournville chocolate, broken into pieces
1 teaspoon sunflower oil
2 tablespoons water
1 oz (25 g) caster sugar

USING THE METAL BLADE

Heat the oven to 350°F/180°C/gas mark 4. Line a 12 × 9 inch (30 × 23 cm) roasting tin with foil and grease the foil lightly.

Measure all the ingredients for the cake into the processor bowl and process for a few seconds to blend. Pour the mixture into the tin and bake in the oven for about 30 minutes, until the cake springs back when lightly pressed with a finger. Leave to cool in the tin.

For the icing, put the chocolate, oil, water and sugar in a small pan and heat very gently until the chocolate has melted. Remove from the heat and beat well until smooth. Pour over the cooled cake and level out evenly.

Lemon Crunchy Loaves

MAKES 2 LOAVES

Making a cake in a loaf tin enables you to produce neat and tidy slices. Bake two at a time, and you can eat one and freeze the other. Alternatively, bake the mixture in a small roasting tin as a traybake. If there is no icing sugar in the store cupboard, use caster or granulated instead for the icing.

4 oz (100 g) soft margarine
6 oz (175 g) self-raising flour
1 level teaspoon baking powder

mon

sugar

USING THE BLADE

°C/gas mark 4. Grease and line two 1 lb greaseproof paper.
our, baking powder, sugar, eggs, milk and bowl and process for a few seconds to mix. e bowl, then reprocess just for a moment. the prepared tins and level out evenly. it 35 minutes, until the cakes have shrunk e tins and spring back when lightly pressed

g, put the lemon juice and sugar for the icing ded. When the loaves come out of the oven, the top while they are still hot. Leave in the urn out, remove the paper and store in an

w even if you don't know all the answers.

O N M L K J I

Grandmother's Rock Cakes

MAKES 24 ROCK
CAKES

If you like, make smaller rock cakes and remember to reduce the cooking
time.

> 8 oz (225 g) self-raising flour
> 2 teaspoons baking powder
> 4 oz (100 g) soft margarine
> 2 oz (50 g) granulated sugar
> 1 egg, beaten
> about 2 tablespoons milk
> 3 oz (75 g) sultanas
> 3 oz (75 g) currants
> a little demerara sugar

USING THE METAL
BLADE

Heat the oven to 400°F/200°C/gas mark 6 and lightly grease two large
baking sheets.

Measure the flour, baking powder, margarine, sugar, egg and milk
into the processor bowl and process for about 10 seconds to mix. This
should be a stiff mixture. Scrape down the sides of the bowl, add the
sultanas and currants and process just long enough to mix in. Spoon out
12 rock cakes on each baking sheet using two teaspoons. Sprinkle each
with demerara sugar.

Put the two trays one above the other in the oven and bake for about
15 minutes, until just beginning to brown at the edges. Swap the trays
over half way through the cooking time. Lift the rock cakes on to a wire
rack to cool.

Butter Shortbread

MAKES 12 FINGERS

The secret of a good shortbread is to use butter for its flavour and to cook
the shortbread until it is the same colour on the bottom as on the top.

> 4 oz (100 g) butter, softened
> 2 oz (50 g) caster sugar
> 4 oz (100 g) flour
> 2 oz (50 g) cornflour, or semolina
> demerara sugar

USING THE METAL
BLADE

Heat the oven to 325°F/160°C/gas mark 3 and lightly grease a shallow 7 inch (17.5 cm) square tin. Measure all the ingredients except the demerara sugar into the processor bowl and process until the mixture forms a ball round the blade. Press the mixture into the tin, level the top and prick all over with a fork. Sprinkle generously with demerara sugar. Bake in the oven for about an hour, until pale golden top and bottom. Don't be afraid to leave it in longer if the bottom is not quite golden.

Cut the shortbread into fingers with a knife and leave in the tin until cold. Lift out the fingers with a palette knife and store in a tin.

Carrot Cake

A really lovely moist cake with a wonderful topping.

4 oz (100 g) carrots
2 oz (50 g) shelled walnuts
8 oz (225 g) self-raising flour
2 level teaspoons baking powder
5 oz (150 g) light soft brown sugar
2 ripe bananas, cut into pieces
2 eggs
¼ pint (150 ml) sunflower oil

TOPPING
3 oz (75 g) soft margarine
3 oz (75 g) cream cheese
6 oz (175 g) icing sugar, sieved
½ teaspoon vanilla essence

USING THE COARSE
GRATING DISC:
METAL BLADE

Heat the oven to 350°F/180°C/gas mark 4. Grease and line an 8 inch (20 cm) round cake tin.

Grate the carrots in the processor and set aside. Fit the metal blade and roughly chop the nuts. Add the remaining cake ingredients and the grated carrots to the processor bowl and process for 40 seconds. Scrape down the sides and process again until well combined.

Turn into the prepared tin and bake for about 1¼ hours, until the cake is golden brown and shrinking slightly from the sides of the tin. A warm skewer inserted in the centre should come out clean. Turn out, remove the lining paper and leave to cool on a wire rack.

Put all the ingredients for the topping in the processor bowl and process until smooth. Scrape down the sides and process again for a few seconds. Spread the topping on to the cake and roughen the surface with a fork. Leave in a cool place for the icing to harden a little before serving.

Lemon Finger Biscuits

MAKES ABOUT
24 BISCUITS

These light crisp biscuits are perfect served with coffee and also make a good accompaniment to mousses and ice creams.

> *4 oz (100 g) soft margarine*
> *4 oz (100 g) butter*
> *2 oz (50 g) icing sugar*
> *8 oz (225 g) plain flour*
> *grated rind of 1 lemon*

USING THE METAL
BLADE

Heat the oven to 325°F/160°C/gas mark 3. Lightly grease 3 baking sheets.

Measure all the ingredients into the processor bowl and process to give a soft dough. Spoon into a piping bag fitted with a ½ inch (1.25 cm) star-shaped nozzle and pipe the mixture on to the baking sheets in 3 inch (7.5 cm) fingers, leaving space in between for them to spread.

Bake in the oven for about 20 minutes, until they are just tinged with golden brown at the edges. Leave to cool for a few moments, then lift on to a wire rack to finish cooling.

Scotch Pancakes

MAKES ABOUT
24 PANCAKES

When you have a crowd for tea but an empty cake tin and little in the larder, make these pancakes and serve with home-made jam or honey.

> *4 oz (100 g) self-raising flour*
> *1 oz (25 g) caster sugar*
> *1 egg*
> *¼ pint (150 ml) milk*
> *oil for frying*

USING THE METAL
BLADE

Measure all the ingredients into the processor bowl. Process for about 10 seconds, scrape down the sides of the bowl and reprocess very briefly.

Heat a heavy frying pan and brush with a little oil. Put tablespoons of mixture into the hot pan, about three or four at a time, spaced apart. When bubbles come to the surface, turn the pancakes over to cook the other side. When set and lightly coloured, lift out on to a cooling rack. Continue until all the batter is used up.

Bread Rolls

MAKES 16 ROLLS

Good to eat and fast to make. Top with cracked wheat, sesame seeds or porridge oats if liked.

2 teaspoons dried yeast
¼ pint (150 ml) milk, hand-hot
¼ pint (150 ml) water, hand-hot
1 teaspoon sugar
8 oz (225 g) strong plain flour
8 oz (225 g) wholemeal flour
1 teaspoon salt
1½ oz (40 g) butter

USING THE METAL BLADE

Put the yeast in a jug and add the milk, water and sugar. Mix well and leave to stand for 10 minutes, until a froth is beginning to form on the surface.

Measure the flour and salt into the processor bowl, add the butter and process for a few seconds to rub in. With the machine running, pour in the yeast liquid through the funnel and process until a dough forms. Continue to process for about 10 seconds to knead the dough. Turn into a bowl, cover with oiled clear film and leave for about ¾ hour, until doubled in size.

Divide the dough into 16 pieces. Knead and roll each piece and put on to greased baking sheets, leaving space between the rolls. Cover loosely with oiled clear film and leave to prove for about 1 hour until doubled in size.

Heat the oven to 450°F/230°C/gas mark 8. Remove the clear film, dust the rolls with flour, and bake in the oven for 12–15 minutes. When cooked they should sound hollow if tapped underneath. Cool on a wire rack.

Traditional Wheatmeal Bread

MAKES 1 LOAF

Using half wholemeal and half plain flour gives a lighter loaf than using just wholemeal flour. If you use a modern fast-acting yeast, follow the packet instructions.

½ pint (300 ml) water, hand-hot
1 teaspoon sugar
1½ teaspoons dried yeast
8 oz (225 g) wholemeal flour
8 oz (225 g) strong plain flour
1 teaspoon salt
1 tablespoon oil

USING THE METAL
BLADE

Dissolve the sugar in the water, sprinkle on the yeast, and leave for 10 minutes, until frothy.

Measure the flours, salt and oil into the processor bowl. With the machine running, pour in the yeast mixture through the funnel and process for about 10 seconds, until a ball of dough forms. Process for a further 45 seconds to knead.

Place the dough in an oiled polythene bag and leave in a warm place for about 1½ hours, until doubled in size.

Return the dough to the processor bowl and process for about 15 seconds. Turn on to a floured surface and shape into a large sausage. Place the dough in a well-greased 1 lb (450 g) loaf tin and put the tin into a polythene bag. Leave to prove in a warm place for about 1 hour. The dough will have risen to the top of the tin.

Heat the oven to 425°F/220°C/gas mark 7. Remove the plastic bag and bake the loaf in the oven for 30–40 minutes. When cooked, it will sound hollow if tapped on the base. Turn out of the tin and cool on a wire rack.

Preserves

The mincing, chopping and slicing involved in making some preserves are all lengthy tasks to do by hand. But with a processor, preserves are quicker and more fun to make. Without doubt one of the most successful ways of making marmalade is to cook the fresh or frozen fruit whole, then to chop the peel in the processor. This method ensures that a firm set is quickly achieved.

If you have any rather hard, stoned dried dates, put them through the processor and they can then be used with windfall apples to make chutney (page 110). To make maximum use of windfalls in late autumn, cook them with the minimum of water, then purée in the processor and freeze in empty yoghurt or cream cartons. You can use the purée in sauces and apple tarts all winter long.

Whole-Fruit Seville Marmalade

MAKES ABOUT 4 LB
(1.8 KG)

This marmalade can be just as easily made from frozen Seville oranges if you didn't have the time or inclination to make it when the fruit came into the shops. Cook the frozen oranges without thawing first. The fruit is cooked whole, then the skins are sliced in the processor. You may need to put it through the processor slicer more than once to obtain the most satisfactory results.

1½ lb (675 g) Seville oranges
juice of 1 lemon
2 pints (1 litre) water
3 lb (1.25 kg) granulated sugar

USING THE COARSE
SLICING DISC

Put the oranges and lemon juice in a large pan and cover with water. Weight the oranges down with a plate if they bob up to the surface. Bring to the boil, cover and simmer for about 1 hour, until the skins are tender. When the fruit is cooked, lift out and drain in a colander over a bowl. Return the liquid to the pan.

When cool enough to handle, cut the oranges in half. Scoop out the flesh and pips and add to the liquid in the saucepan. Bring to the boil and cook for 6 minutes without a lid. Strain the liquid through a sieve to remove the pips and flesh, pressing with a spoon to extract all the liquid. Save the liquid.

Cut the halved orange skins in half again. Fit as many orange skin quarters as possible into the processor funnel, insert the plastic pusher and switch on: pressing the fruit skins down will ensure that the slices are as straight as possible. Return the sliced skins to the liquid in the pan, add the sugar and stir over a low heat until the sugar is dissolved completely. Turn up the heat and boil rapidly for 10–15 minutes, until setting point is reached.

To test for setting, take a teaspoon of the marmalade and place it on a cold saucer. Let it cool, then push the skin that forms. If it has set the skin should wrinkle. If not set enough, boil for a few more minutes and test again. When setting point is reached, draw off the heat and skim any scum. Leave in the pan to cool for 10 minutes, then pot, seal and label.

Variations

Ginger Marmalade
Add 4 oz (100 g) chopped stem ginger after the sugar has dissolved. This is a good way to use up the half jar of ginger which sits in the cupboard after Christmas!

Dark Vintage Marmalade
Add 4 oz (100 g) dark muscovado sugar and subtract 4 oz (100 g) of white sugar from the original ingredients. If you add more than that amount of muscovado, the marmalade may go syrupy.

Three-Fruit Marmalade

MAKES ABOUT 5 LB
(2.25 KG)

So quick and easy to make in the processor, at any time of the year when you run out of Seville marmalade. It has a good set, because the fruit is chopped finely, and it produces a high yield.

1½ lb (675 g) mixed fruits (oranges, grapefruits, lemons)
juice of 1 lemon
2 pints (1 litre) water
3 lb (1.25 kg) sugar

USING THE METAL
BLADE

Cut the fruits in half and squeeze the juice into a large pan, saving all the pips and pith. Any stubborn pith can be removed from the skin with a teaspoon. Put all the pith and pips in a piece of clean muslin and tie tightly into a bag. Place the bag in the pan. Cut the fruit halves into quarters and process to the chunkiness preferred. Add to the pan with the extra lemon juice and pour on the water. Bring to the boil, cover with a lid and simmer until the peel is tender.

Remove the bag of pips from the pan, squeezing out as much juice as possible. Add the sugar and stir until it has dissolved, then turn up the heat and bring to a full boil. Cook for about 10 minutes, then test for a set. To do this, put a teaspoon of marmalade on a cold saucer. Leave for a few minutes to cool, then push the skin that forms. If it has set the skin should wrinkle. If not set enough, boil for another few minutes and test again. Allow to cool for about 10 minutes, then pot and seal.

Peanut Butter

MAKES ONE
SMALL JAR

The choice of peanuts is entirely personal, but dry-roasted give the most traditional taste. No sugar or other sweetening is necessary. To vary the flavour you can add some almonds or hazelnuts to the peanuts.

6 oz (175 g) roasted salted peanuts
1–1½ tablespoons sunflower oil

USING THE METAL
BLADE

Measure the peanuts into the processor bowl, then with machine running pour in the oil through the funnel, a little at a time, until you have the texture you like. The less oil you use, the smoother the end result will be.

Apple, Pepper and Date Chutney

MAKES ABOUT
4 LB (1.8 KG)

An economical chutney using windfall apples and peppers when they are cheap and plentiful. If the apples are small there is no need to peel them.

2 lb (900 g) cooking apples, cored and cut into quarters
2 red peppers, halved and seeded
4 oz (100 g) stoned dates
½ oz (15 g) fresh ginger root
¼ oz (10 g) mixed pickling spice
1 tablespoon salt
1 teaspoon whole mixed spices
¾ pint (450 ml) distilled malt vinegar
1 lb (450 g) light muscovado sugar

USING THE METAL
BLADE: COARSE
GRATING DISC

Put the apples in the processor bowl and chop them coarsely. Chop the peppers in the same way, then the dates. Fit the grating disc and grate the ginger. Tie the pickling spice in a piece of muslin.

Put all the ingredients in a large pan, heat slowly until the sugar has dissolved, then bring to the boil. Simmer for 30–40 minutes until thick, stirring from time to time to prevent sticking.

Pot, seal and label.

Pickled Red Cabbage

MAKES 3 JARS

Salting the cabbage overnight is the secret to crisp pickled cabbage.

1 medium-sized firm red cabbage, about 2 lb (900 g)
4 level tablespoons salt
3 pints (1.75 litres) distilled malt vinegar
1 oz (25 g) soft brown sugar

USING THE FINE
SLICING DISC

Cut the cabbage into chunks, then slice in the processor. Arrange layers of cabbage in a bowl, sprinkling salt on each layer. Cover and leave overnight.

Pour the vinegar into a saucepan with the sugar. Heat gently to dissolve the sugar, then leave to cool.

Drain the cabbage, rinse off the surplus salt and drain thoroughly. Pack into jars with vinegar-proof seals and pour in the cold vinegar. Seal and label the jars.

Store in a cool, dark larder and use within 4 months. If kept longer, it loses its crispness and colour.

Cucumber Dill Pickle

MAKES 3 JARS

Serve with cold meats or fish.

3 large cucumbers
4 tablespoons salt
8 oz (225 g) granulated sugar
1 pint (600 ml) distilled malt vinegar
2 tablespoons dried dill

USING THE COARSE
SLICING DISC

Slice the cucumbers in the processor. Transfer to a bowl and sprinkle with the salt. Leave for 2 hours, then rinse and drain thoroughly.

Measure the sugar and vinegar into a pan, bring to the boil and simmer for about 3 minutes.

Pack the cucumber into warm jars, sprinkling the dill in between the layers. Cover with the vinegar and seal immediately. Use within 2 months.

Pesto

MAKES 1 JAR

Capture the essence of Italy by making your own pesto. Fresh basil is essential. Add pesto to vegetables, sauces and soups or serve in the traditional way, stirred into hot freshly cooked pasta. Use it on baked potatoes, too, instead of butter. If you make larger quantities, keep in jars covered with a layer of olive oil and then a good screw top. Pesto also freezes well.

2 oz (50 g) Parmesan cheese
2 oz (50 g) basil leaves, stalks removed
large fat clove garlic, crushed
salt
1 oz (25 g) pine nuts
3–4 fl oz (90–120 ml) olive oil

USING THE FINE GRATING DISC: METAL BLADE

Grate the Parmesan in the processor and set aside.

Fit the metal blade. Put the basil, garlic, salt and pine nuts in the processor bowl and process until smooth. Scrape down the sides of the bowl, add the cheese and process again. With the machine running, add the oil in a thin stream through the funnel, processing until the consistency is like creamed butter.

Store in a jar in the refrigerator and use within 3 months.

Fresh Horseradish

If you have horseradish in the garden it will flourish for ever. In fact it is considered by many to be a weed! Once the roots are peeled, process at once and then bottle, to prevent discolouring. To make horseradish sauce for serving with meat or fish, drain the vinegar and add the horseradish to fresh cream or condensed milk.

horseradish roots
cider vinegar
salt
sugar

USING THE METAL BLADE

Wash the horseradish roots and scrape or peel the skin. Cut the roots into chunky pieces and process until finely chopped. Take care when removing the processor lid – the pungent aroma may make your eyes water!

Pack small or medium-sized screw-top jars two-thirds full. Add ½ teaspoon salt and 1 teaspoon sugar to each jar. Cover with vinegar, seal and label.

Keeps for up to 6 months.

Mint Sauce Concentrate

MAKES ½ PINT (300 ML) CONCENTRATE

Pick garden mint at its best, just before flowering. It will shoot again in a short time.

> *8 oz (225 g) granulated sugar*
> *½ pint (300 ml) distilled malt vinegar*
> *6 oz (175 g) fresh mint leaves*

USING THE METAL BLADE

Put the sugar and vinegar in a pan and bring to the boil. Chop the mint in the processor. With the machine running, carefully pour in the hot liquid through the funnel and process until the mint is fine and mixed with the liquid.

Pour into screw-top jars or bottles and use diluted with extra vinegar for mint sauce.

Good Things to go with Drinks

*H*ome-made savouries are a bonus. I try to make 'eats' such as Flaky Cheese Crisps (page 118), Cashew Nutters (page 117) and Mini Quiches (page 121) in a double quantity so that I have some to freeze. Then if a couple of friends drop in for a drink I can whip some out of the freezer and reheat them in 10 minutes or so. Ideally they should be thawed before reheating, if time allows.

You can make your own potato crisps using the processor's fine slicing disc. Put the potato slices in cold water for 10 minutes to rinse off excess starch, then drain, dry and fry in deep fat until golden.

Avocado Dip

SERVES 6

Serve this with an attractive selection of crisp fresh vegetables for dunking – such as fingers of cucumbers and carrot, sprigs of calebrese and cauliflower, strips of pepper, chicory leaves and whole small mushrooms.

> *2 ripe avocado pears*
> *juice of 1 large lemon*
> *1 tablespoon oil*
> *½ teaspoon made English mustard*
> *1 teaspoon caster sugar*
> *salt*
> *freshly ground black pepper*
> *¼ pint (150 ml) Greek yoghurt*

USING THE METAL BLADE

Cut the avocado pears in half and remove the stones and skin. Put the avocado flesh in the processor bowl with all the remaining ingredients and process until creamy and smooth. Scrape down the sides of the bowl and process again briefly. Taste and check seasoning.

Turn into a small bowl, place on a large plate and surround with fresh vegetables.

Spiced Mango and Cheese Dip

SERVES 6

A delicious dip to go with drinks, served with potato crisps or vegetables. See Avocado Dip (above) for ideas.

> *4 tablespoons mango chutney*
> *2 teaspoons Dijon mustard*
> *1 teaspoon curry powder*
> *8 oz (225 g) cream cheese*
> *milk, for thinning*

USING THE METAL BLADE

Put all the ingredients except the milk in the processor bowl and process until smooth. Scrape down the sides of the bowl and check the consistency. If it is too stiff, add a little milk and reprocess briefly.

Turn into a bowl and surround with crisps or vegetables.

Home-Made Garlic Herb Cheese

SERVES 4–6

Garnish with fresh herbs and serve as part of a cheeseboard. You can then use the last scraps for a sandwich filling.

2 spring onions
a handful of fresh parsley sprigs
leaves from 2 sprigs of thyme and 2 sprigs of tarragon
salt
freshly ground black pepper
8 oz (225 g) rich cream cheese
2 cloves garlic, crushed
a little top of the milk

USING THE METAL BLADE

Put the spring onions and herbs in the processor bowl and chop finely. Add all the other ingredients except the milk and switch on briefly to mix, adding a little milk if necessary to give a spreading consistency. Taste and check seasoning.

Pile the mixture into a dish, cover and refrigerate until needed.

Cheese Savouries

MAKES ABOUT 15 BALLS

These need to be chilled before serving so that they will hold their shape well.

8 oz (225 g) well-flavoured Cheddar cheese
4 oz (100 g) shelled walnuts
a little oil
about 1½ tablespoons mayonnaise (page 67)
salt
freshly ground black pepper

USING THE COARSE
GRATING DISC:
METAL BLADE

Grate the cheese in the processor and set aside.

Toast the walnuts in a heavy frying pan, adding just enough oil to coat the base thinly. Keep turning and moving the walnuts until they are an even brown colour. Drain on kitchen paper and leave to cool. When cool, fit the metal blade and chop the nuts roughly in the processor. Transfer to a plate.

Put the grated cheese in the processor bowl and process with sufficient mayonnaise to bind. Season to taste.

Take teaspoons of mixture and form into balls, then roll in the toasted walnuts.

Cashew Nutters

MAKES ABOUT 40

These are one of my great standbys – crisp cheese savouries that are quickly made. They freeze well, too. If you hate piping, allow the mixture to become firm in the fridge then roll it into small balls. Flatten the balls and press a nut in the top of each, then bake.

3 oz (75 g) matured Cheddar cheese
4 oz (100 g) soft margarine, slightly warmed but not melted
2 oz (50 g) semolina
3½ oz (90 g) self-raising flour
salt
freshly ground black pepper
½ teaspoon dry mustard
about 40 unsalted cashew nut halves or blanched almond halves

USING THE FINE
GRATING DISC:
METAL BLADE

Heat the oven to 350°F/180°C/gas mark 4. Grate the cheese in the processor.

Fit the metal blade, put all the ingredients except the nuts in the processor bowl and process until a soft dough forms. Take a large piping bag fitted with a ½ inch (1.25 cm) plain nozzle and pipe about 40 small blobs on a large baking sheet. Press a half nut into the centre of each one.

Bake in the oven for 15–20 minutes, until pale golden brown. Cool on a wire rack, then store in an airtight tin.

Flaky Cheese Crisps

MAKES ABOUT
100 CHEESE CRISPS

These take a little time to make so it is really worthwhile making the amount of pastry given here and freezing what you don't need. Then just slice the crisps from the thawed raw pastry block and bake them. Bake in batches on silicone paper to prevent sticking and re-use the paper for all the batches. Watch them in the oven as they burn easily.

8 oz (225 g) well-flavoured dry Cheddar cheese
2 oz (50 g) Parmesan cheese
12 oz (350 g) hard margarine, well chilled
1 lb (450 g) strong plain flour
1 teaspoon dry mustard
salt
about ½ pint (300 ml) cold water

USING THE FINE
GRATING DISC:
COARSE GRATING
DISC: METAL BLADE

Grate the cheeses in the processor using the fine grating disc and set aside. Fit the coarse grating disc and grate the chilled margarine. Put it in the fridge to stop it softening.

Fit the metal blade. Measure the flour, mustard and salt into the processor bowl, add the chilled margarine and some of the water and process briefly, adding more water through the funnel until the mixture forms a dough. Switch off immediately. Be careful not to overprocess or the pastry will not be flaky.

Roll the dough into an oblong on a floured board. Divide the mixed grated cheeses into four piles. Sprinkle one quarter of the cheese over two thirds of the pastry, then fold twice as if you were making puff pastry. Wrap in clear film and chill in the refrigerator for 15 minutes. Roll out and repeat the process three more times so that all the cheese is used up. wrap and chill for at least 2 hours but preferably overnight.

Heat the oven to 425°F/220°C/gas mark 7 and line some baking sheets with silicone paper. Take the block of cheese pastry and cut off ⅛ inch (3 mm) slices. Lay the slices flat so you can see the flaky layers and cut them into ½ inch (4 cm) pieces. Arrange them carefully on the baking sheets and bake in the oven for about 10 minutes, until golden brown and crisp, turning once half way through the cooking time.

Prawn Roulades

MAKES ABOUT
100 SLICES

These look amazingly professional and taste delicious, too.

PÂTÉ
5 oz (150 g) butter, melted
4 oz (100 g) rich cream cheese
2 tablespoons tomato purée
juice of ½ lemon
freshly ground black pepper
6 oz (175 g) shelled prawns

1 uncut firm brown loaf
parsley, to garnish

USING THE METAL
BLADE

Put all pâté ingredients except the prawns in the processor bowl and process until smooth. Add the prawns and process for just a few moments, so they retain some texture, then taste and check seasoning. Transfer to a bowl.

Cut the crusts off the loaf. Using a sharp knife slice carefully into ⅛ inch (3 mm) slices along the length of the loaf. Spread the pâté generously on each slice and roll up the slices like Swiss rolls. Wrap each roll in clear film and chill well.

To serve, unwrap the rolls and cut each one into about 16 slices each. Arrange on a plate or tray and garnish with parsley.

Variation

Smoked Salmon Roulades
Replace the prawns with 8 oz (225 g) smoked salmon pieces, processing them with the other ingredients to make a smooth pâté.

Mini Quiches

◆

MAKES ABOUT 24

These tiny tarts are made from rich shortcrust pastry, with an addition of cheese to give more flavour. Good with drinks, they also make a tasty first course. If you don't have tartlet moulds, use mince pie tins.

PASTRY
1 egg yolk
1 tablespoon cold water
6 oz (175 g) plain flour
4 oz (100 g) butter, cut into pieces
2 tablespoons finely grated Parmesan cheese
1 teaspoon mixed fresh leafy herbs (optional)

FILLING
8 oz (225 g) onion
2 oz (50 g) butter
2 eggs
1 egg yolk
salt
freshly ground black pepper
¼ pint (300 ml) double cream

USING THE METAL BLADE

In a bowl, mix together the egg yolk and water for the pastry. Put the flour, butter, cheese and herbs, if using, in the processor bowl and process until the mixture resembles fine breadcrumbs. With the machine running, add the liquid through the funnel and process until the dough forms a ball, but do not overprocess. Wrap the pastry in clear film and chill in the refrigerator for 15 minutes before rolling out.

Heat the oven to 375°F/190°C/gas mark 5 and have ready some small tartlet moulds. Roll the pastry thinly and with a plain cutter cut out rounds a little larger than the moulds. Drop the pastry rounds into the moulds, line with foil and bake blind in the oven for about 10 minutes, removing the foil for the final 5 minutes. Set the pastry cases aside and lower the oven temperature to 325°F/160°C/gas mark 3.

To make the filling, fit the metal blade and finely chop the onion. Sauté the onion in the butter until soft but not coloured, remove from the pan with a draining spoon and put to one side. Measure the remaining filling ingredients into a bowl and whisk together until blended.

Divide the onion among the pastry cases and pour on the egg and cream mixture. Bake in the oven for about 15 minutes, until the filling is set, slightly risen and brown.

Serve hot or cold.

Variations

Smoked Salmon Mini Quiches

Cut up 8 oz (225 g) smoked salmon pieces fairly finely and place in base of the pastry cases. Omit the onion.

Bacon Mini Quiches

Fry 8 oz (225 g) smoked bacon without fat until almost crispy, and place in the base of the pastry cases with the onion.

Cheese Aigrettes

MAKES ABOUT
30 CHOUX BALLS

These little cheese choux pastry balls make an unusual snack to serve with drinks or as part of a buffet. Traditionally they are deep fried, but if they are made a bit smaller you can shallow fry them, turning them once. It is more difficult to judge when the aigrettes are cooked through if you shallow fry, so test one or two to make sure all the inside has cooked. To reheat the aigrettes for a party, arrange them on a baking sheet and heat in the oven at 425°F/220°C/gas mark 7 for about 12 minutes, until thoroughly heated and crispy.

4 oz (100 g) well-flavoured Cheddar cheese
4 oz (100 g) self-raising flour
2 oz (50 g) butter
½ pint (300 ml) water
2 eggs
2 egg yolks
salt
freshly ground black pepper
oil for deep frying

USING THE MEDIUM
GRATING DISC:
METAL BLADE

Grate the cheese in the processor and set to one side.

Fit the metal blade and measure the flour into the processor bowl. Bring the butter and water slowly to the boil in a small pan, ensuring that the butter has melted. With the machine running, pour in the liquid through the funnel and process until smooth, scraping down the sides of the bowl as necessary. Leave to cool.

Mix the eggs and egg yolks together in a jug. With the machine running, pour in the eggs through the funnel and process until the dough is smooth and glossy. Scrape down the sides of the bowl and reprocess very briefly. Add the seasoning and grated cheese and process to mix together.

Drop teaspoons of mixture into deep hot fat, frying until golden brown. Lift out and drain on kitchen paper. Serve warm.

Spicy Samosas

MAKES ABOUT
36 SAMOSAS

Good with drinks, these can also be served as part of a curry meal.

1 onion, cut into quarters
1 clove garlic, crushed
½ inch (1.25 cm) piece fresh ginger root, thinly peeled
2 tablespoons oil
8 oz (225 g) chuck steak
1 tablespoon tomato purée
¼ teaspoon ground turmeric
½ teaspoon garam masala
½ teaspoon ground coriander
3 oz (75 g) small frozen peas or chopped spinach
salt
1 packet filo pastry, thawed
2 oz (50 g) butter, melted

USING THE METAL
BLADE

Chop the onion finely in the processor with the ginger and garlic. Heat some oil in a pan and fry them together until soft.

Process the meat until it is finely minced and add to the onions and garlic. Fry until dry and brown. Mix in the tomato purée and spices and fry for about 2 minutes. Add a little water if needed to prevent the mixture sticking and cook for about 10 minutes. Try not to add too much water as the mixture should be dry. Add the peas or spinach and cook until tender. Season with salt and set aside to cool.

Heat the oven to 375°F/190°C/gas mark 5 and lightly grease a baking sheet. Open the packet of filo pastry. Use one sheet at a time and keep the remaining sheets covered with a damp tea towel to prevent them from drying out.

Cut the first sheet of filo into about five long strips and brush each strip with melted butter. At the top of one strip place a teaspoon of the meat mixture, then fold the pastry over the meat to form a triangle (top left corner over meat to right-hand side of pastry). Fold the triangle over again, keeping its three-cornered shape, and continue this process until you reach the end of the strip and the filo is several layers thick. Repeat with the remaining meat mixture and filo.

Arrange the samosas on the baking sheet. Brush with melted butter and bake for about 15 minutes, until nicely brown. Serve warm.

Drinks

$\diamond$

Children enjoy all sorts of concoctions whizzed up in the processor. Our young especially like ice cream sodas: just fresh soft fruit, such as strawberries or bananas, processed together with chilled lemonade then poured into a tall glass, topped with a scoop of strawberry or vanilla ice cream and served with a long-handled spoon.

Chilled milk with puréed fresh fruit makes a quick and nutritious milkshake. And a good Whole Lemon Drink (page 124) can be made in the processor with little effort.

This year we made four gallons of elderflower cordial to make Elderflower Champagne (page 125). It has been popular with all ages. I serve it as an alternative to Pimms on a summer's day when friends have to be in the driving seat at the end of the day.

Crushed ice is easy to prepare in the processor – simply process the ice until it is the desired consistency. For coloured frosting to decorate glasses, put sugar in the processor bowl and add a few drops of vegetable colouring. Process briefly until the colour is even.

Strawberry Yoghurt Drink

SERVES 3

Children seem to adore yoghurt drinks. Home-made ones are far better than bought. See page 66 for tips on making fruit purées.

⅓ pint (200 ml) strawberry purée, chilled
⅔ pint (400 ml) natural yoghurt, chilled
sugar to taste

USING THE METAL BLADE

Measure the purée and yoghurt into a processor and process until smooth. Add sugar to taste. Pour into individual glasses and serve straight away with ice.

Variations

Pineapple or Cherry Yoghurt Drink
As a change use pineapple or cherry purée and make exactly as above.

Raspberry Yoghurt Drink
If you want to use raspberry purée, sieve it first to remove the pips.

Blackberry Yoghurt Drink
Blackberries need cooking before they're puréed and the purée must also be sieved.

Whole Lemon Drink

MAKES 1 PINT
(600 ML)

This is a spur-of-the-moment drink, made quickly. Serve with ice and mint. It should be used fairly soon as it does not keep long.

1 lemon, cut into quarters
1 pint (600 ml) cold water
1–2 tablespoons caster sugar, to taste

USING THE METAL BLADE

Place the lemon in the processor bowl. With the machine running, add the water through the feed tube, then sugar to taste. Continue until the fruit is finely processed.
  Strain into a jug and serve chilled.

Elderflower Champagne

◆

MAKES 2½ PINTS
(1.5 LITRES)
CONCENTRATE

How can Champagne be non-boosey? Well this one is! Keep the cordial in the refrigerator for up to 3 months.

> *3½ lb (1.6 kg) granulated sugar*
> *2½ pints (1.5 litres) water*
> *3 lemons*
> *25 elderflower heads*
> *2 oz (50 g) citric acid*
> *chilled sparkling water and ice, to serve*

USING THE COARSE
SLICING DISC

Measure the sugar and water into a large pan. Bring to the boil, stirring occasionally to dissolve the sugar, then remove from heat and allow to cool.

Slice the lemons in the processor and put them in a polythene box (an old ice cream carton will do) with the citric acid and elderflower heads. Pour over the cold syrup, cover and leave in a cold place overnight. Strain the cordial into bottles and store in the refrigerator.

To serve, dilute to taste with chilled sparkling water and ice.

Quick Drinks

◆

ALL SERVE 4

Made in no time!

USING THE METAL
BLADE

Banana Milkshake
Put two bananas into the processor, add 1 pint (600 ml) chilled milk and process until smooth. Pour into glasses and serve chilled.

Iced Coffee
Measure 2 tablespoons coffee essence into the processor, add 1 pint (600 ml) chilled milk and process until well blended. Pour into glasses and serve with ice.

Index